Frank E. Huggett read history at Wadham College, Oxford, and then worked for a national newspaper in Fleet Street for three years. In 1952 he gave up journalism to become a full-time author and has written many books on social history, including *Life Below Stairs, Life and Work at Sea* and *A Day in the Life of a Victorian Farm Labourer*. He has also written scripts for the B.B.C. on the Victorian age and has lectured on journalism in this country and abroad.

VICTORIAN ENGLAND AS SEEN BY PUNCH

PUBLISHED EVERY SATURDAY.

PRICE THREEPENCE. STAMPED 4d.

N° 765.
VOLUME
THE
THIRTIETH.
MARCH 8,
1856.

PUNCH OFFICE, 85, FLEET STREET.
AND SOLD BY ALL BOOKSELLERS.

Frank E. Huggett

VICTORIAN ENGLAND
as seen by
PUNCH

Sidgwick & Jackson
London

First published in Great Britain in 1978 by
Sidgwick & Jackson Limited. Edited and produced by
Book Club Associates

© Frank E. Huggett 1978

Designed by Harold Bartram

Set in Monophoto Century Schoolbook
and printed by Jarrold and Sons Ltd, Norwich,
for Sidgwick & Jackson Limited,
1 Tavistock Chambers, Bloomsbury Way,
London WC1A 2SG.

ISBN 0 283 98488 0

CONTENTS

1 RADICAL OVERTURES

1841–1846

Long before the Victorian age came to a close, Punch had become a pillar of the middle-class establishment and a national institution; but in the first few tentative years of its metropolitan existence, it was a very different kind of periodical, a staunch defender of the poor and the oppressed and a radical scourge of all authority. Punch was born on July 17, 1841, four years and a month after Queen Victoria came to the throne, as a self-styled 'guffawgraph' and a 'refuge for destitute wit, an asylum for the thousands of orphan jokes, the millions of perishing puns, which are now wandering about without so much as a shelf to rest upon'. It could be comic, ridiculous, droll, jocular, urbane, facetious, witty, though never salacious, as it was a family paper from the start; but there was also a far more serious element as Mark Lemon, one of the co-editors, observed in the very first article in the first issue, 'The Moral of Punch'. Their eponymous, hook-nosed, hump-backed hero was distinguished not only for his 'rude and boisterous mirth', but also for his ability as 'a teacher of no mean pretensions'. His cudgel had pointed out the original targets of their own abuse, those visual and oral cheats by whom mankind had always been cajoled: the nobleman in his robes and coronet; the dignitary in the fulness of his pomp; the demagogue in the triumph of his

---

SOME CONUNDRUMS AND 'PERISHING PUNS'

Why is the common chord in music like a portion of the Mediterranean Sea?—Because it's the E G & C (Aegean Sea).
When a person holds an argument with his neighbour on the opposite side of the street, why is there no chance of their agreeing?—Because they argue from different *premises*.

Keeping it Dark

Jim Bones, a free nigger of New York, has a child so exceedingly dark that he cannot be seen on the lightest day.
When is Peel not Peel?—When he's candi(e)d.
Why are abbots the greatest dunces in the world?—Because they never get further than their Abbacy (A,B,C).
'Never saw such *stirring* times,' as the spoon said to the saucepan.
Why is an auctioneer like a man with an ugly countenance?—Because he is always for-bidding.
There is at present a man in New York whose temper is so exceedingly hot that he invariably reduces all his shirts to tinder.

1841

THE LIONS OF LONDON

Punch's Guide to the Metropolis

Promenade concerts, instrumental and vocal, take place daily in the streets. The former, consisting of a cornopean, harp and violin, are usually held towards dusk in front of retail wine-vaults.

The British Museum. This admirable building is full of everything curious, from an elephant's tusk to the magnified leg of a bluebottle.

The Government Offices. Are the temporary residences of numerous patriotic gentlemen who are anxious to serve their country— at from £75 to £5,000 per annum. They are generally very snug berths, and are pleasantly situated in the vicinity of the parks, thus rendering one of the duties of the *employés*—that of looking out of window—less arduous and irksome.

The Thames. When analysed Father Thames is found to consist of

Pure water .... 4 parts
Miscellaneous .... 96 parts

This water is considered by the inhabitants of London a most delicious beverage, and they all pay certain companies (who lay it on uncommonly thick) for the privilege of drinking it.

Buckingham Palace. As it is desirable that the Sovereign should always overlook the people, there is one wing of the Palace which commands the whole of the first and second floors of the houses in Victoria Street, and the royal party can at all times observe what is passing in the tap of the Gun Tavern.

The House of Commons. The benches in the House of Commons are remarkable for their narcotic properties, and many members, who are said to be particularly wide-awake to their own interests, have been known to sleep soundly throughout a debate which has involved the happiness of thousands.

The Bridges. Westminster Bridge is a remarkable structure; for it has been tumbling to pieces ever since it was originally built: and it is a singular fact, that as soon as one arch is rendered safe, another is discovered to be dangerous.

Westminster Abbey. This splendid specimen of Gothic architecture has for some years been converted into a raree-show by the Dean and Chapter, who are entrusted with the care of it. The interior is considered to be of so sacred a character, that none are admitted to it who cannot afford to pay threepence.

Mock Auctions. They generally present a large assortment of showy and tempting articles, whose real value is determined by what they will fetch. The casual visitor has only to wink his eye, rub his nose, yawn, sneeze, or cough, and he is sure to find himself the fortunate purchaser of a pair of elegant cut-glass decanters, which cannot be matched—even by one another.

The Thames Tunnel. Is a large bricked tube which passes under the bed of the stream. The purpose for which it was constructed has never been clearly ascertained, but some highly scientific individuals have conceived that during a severe winter it is intended to be filled with boiling water, and so ensure the uninterrupted navigation of the river, by preventing an accumulation of ice.

1842

Previous page: The northern side of Trafalgar Square in the 1840s or early 1850s with a 'Peeler' talking to two passers by

hollowness; and the hangman who assumed a right which was purely providential. 'Punch hangs the devil', Lemon wrote. 'This is as it should be.'

Most of the early contributors were youngish men, around thirty years of age, ambitious, talented, but still not firmly established in their careers or in society. They included Henry Mayhew, who produced the classic investigation of the lives of London's labouring classes and the poor after he had severed his connections with the magazine; Gilbert Abbott à Beckett, who later, as one of the Poor Law Commissioners, wrote the report on the scandal at Andover workhouse where paupers had been forced to gnaw animal bones just to keep alive; and Douglas Jerrold, described as 'that savage little Robespierre' by Thackeray, another early contributor.

Some of these writers, and a number of the artists, too, had experienced a traumatic fall in family fortunes in their youth, which helped to stimulate their sympathy for those who had suffered other misfortunes. But the early radicalism had a far more substantial and general basis stretching back to the beginning of the nineteenth century, when both the working and the middle classes had been allied in their fight against the 'old corruption' of the landed aristocracy, and in their demands for parliamentary reform. This bond was virtually broken when the First Reform Act of 1832 gave the vote to the middle classes, but excluded the workers by making the franchise dependent on a property qualification. The working classes had to continue their fight against the establishment by other means, the Chartist movement;

THE STATISTICAL SOCIETY

This useful Society will shortly publish its Report; and, though we have not seen it, we are entitled to guess with tolerable accuracy what will be the contents of it.

In the first place, we shall be told the number of pins picked up in the course of a day by a person walking over a space of fifteen miles round London, with the number of those not picked up; an estimate of the class of persons that have probably dropped them, with the use they were being put to when they actually fell; and how they have been applied afterwards.

The Report will also put the public in possession of the number of potboys employed in London; what is the average number of pots they carry out; and what is the gross weight of metal in the pots brought back again.

There are also to be published with the report elaborate tables, showing how many quarts of milk are spilt in the course of a year serving customers; what proportion of water it contains; and what are the average ages and breed of the dogs who lap it up; and how much is left unlapped to be absorbed in the atmosphere.

When this valuable Report is published, we shall make copious extracts.

1841

---

but in this new struggle they were supported by only a smaller number of middle-class militants.

In its early years, Punch reflected the minority middle-class view and regularly clubbed and pummelled members of the establishment, both high and low, including Prince Albert; lords of all degrees and their gold-braided flunkeys; the prime minister, Sir Robert Peel, dubbed 'Sir Rhubarb Pill, M.P., M.D., the new state physician', who reintroduced the income tax in 1842 for a temporary three-year period which has lasted ever since; MPs of all parties, or of none, who needed neither honesty nor education to succeed, but only a sufficient stock of impudence and humbug; and the Lord Mayor of London and the corporation, who feasted on real turtle soup while the masses starved.

Queen Victoria, and other members of the Royal Family, were not granted affection and deference; they had to gain it through their own achievements. Personal attacks on the monarchy, which would be considered in bad taste by many people today, were far more general then, and had been even more scurrilous earlier during the Regency period. Punch, like many of its xenophobic readers, could not forgive Prince Albert for having been born a German and could scarcely pardon the Prince of Wales, and his large band of royal brothers and sisters, for having been born at all. The birth of the Prince of Wales (the future Edward VII) in 1841, may have given rise to familial and official rejoicing, but Punch did not share the sycophantic attitudes of some sections of the press. Year after year it chronicled with delighted irony the progress of the royal baby towards infantile maturity. With feigned indignation, it complained that if people had only been less phlegmatic, and more careful of the interests of posterity, the choice of a name for the infant prince would have throbbed in the heart of the whole nation; instead, there had only been some suggestions from the remoter reaches of Wales that he should be called Cadwaller or Llewellyn. Punch's own choice was Lazarus, to confirm that 'suffering and rags and squalor', which were such a characteristic feature of the Hungry Forties, still commanded some sympathy in the royal 'bosom' (not, of course, in a family paper, 'breast').

The official christening was parodied in a mock report of the christening of young Master Cleaver, the heir-apparent to his master's 'shambles', attended by a comic procession of scamps, tramps and blackguards and a squadron of the 8th Baked-Potato Boys. The announcement that the Prince had been weaned, a momentous event unrecorded in the history of any previous Prince of Wales, was seen as a fine augury for the future monarch, who had taken to his pap-spoon with such princely fortitude. Not long afterwards, the Prince was made the colonel of a regiment. Punch, with its proclivity to puns, commented that this was not so preposterous as it might seem, as his Royal Highness would have fitted comfortably into a 'good-sized nut-shell'. The news that the

two-year-old prince was to have his own separate household provoked the suggestion that his establishment might include:

Master of the Rocking Horse
Comptroller of the Juvenile Vagaries
Sugar Stick in Waiting
Captain of the (Tin) Guard
Clerk of the Pea Shooter
Lord Privy Shuttlecock
Quartermaster-General of the Oranges.

Prince Albert, of Saxe-Coburg and Gotha (the biggest royal matrimonial agency in Europe), who had married his cousin, Victoria, in 1840, was even more anathema to Punch, and, initially, at least, to large segments of the middle classes and the establishment. He was derided for his stiff, formal manners and his foreign accent, 'gompliments' instead of 'compliments'; he was suspected of political intrigue, Catholicism and despotic tendencies. His Teutonic passion for uniforms made him a natural butt for the English sense of humour. Not content with decking out his own regiment—the Eleventh Hussars—in scarlet and gold pantaloons, he went on to design a new cap for the whole of the British army which was scathingly dismissed as 'a decided cross between a muff, a coal-scuttle, and a slop pail'. When Prince Albert

The gluttony of London aldermen was a frequent source of amusement in the early days of the magazine. Even when they were ill they could not forgo the pleasure of having their housekeeper read out recipes of the delights they were missing (1843)

was made a freeman of one of the great city livery companies, the Merchant Taylors, in 1845, Punch presented his ironic 'gompliments': the Prince had been 'born with the finest eye for a pattern book, with the boldest hand for the shears. Never did a four-year-old miss dress her dolls with a more fantastic sense of the gaudy and the ludicrous than has the gallant Colonel of the "Prince's Own" tricked out his corps of human playthings.' It was a most appropriate honour which would allow him to 'sit cross-legged in the eyes of posterity'.

The Prince's continental style of huntin' and shootin' made him fair game for further abuse. English lords liked the excitement of the chase; but ease of slaughter was more important on the Continent where stags, the royal quarry, were first caught and then penned into a compound. After one such stag hunt on the Isle of Wight in 1845, Punch wrote a new spelling book to instruct the infant Prince of Wales, in this royal and manly sport:

> The Deer is a poor weak Brute which it is good to kill. It was once the Plan to Hunt the Deer; but it Runs so fast that it puts one quite in a Heat to try to Catch it. A PRINCE should not get Hot, or be at such Pains to Hunt the Deer, but should have all the Deer Caught, and put in a small Space, which they can in no way get Out of. Then the PRINCE should come with his Gun, and Shoot at the Deer when he must kill some!

Later that year when Victoria and Albert made a visit to 'Sacks-Cobug-Gothy', Prince 'Halbert' is shown in a cartoon slitting a stag's throat with a broad-bladed knife while 'Britannia's Queen' looks on from her canopied throne at this 'pore Germing sport' with regal pity.

The Queen got off more lightly, but even she copped it from time to time for her neglect of native talents in the arts; her patronage of French milliners; and her girlish delight in General Tom Thumb—Charles Stratton, the twenty-five-inch high American dwarf—who gave several royal command performances at the Palace in 1844. (Punch's humanitarianism made it dislike exhibitions of freaks just as strongly as the sordid spectacle of public hangings.) The Queen's decision in 1844 to divert all uneaten slices of bread from Prince Albert's pigs to the poor people of Windsor was hailed ironically as a great act of 'royal benevolence'.

Lavish spectacles of royal pomp and ducal splendour aroused Punch's wrath, which became almost apoplectic when royal pensioners and hangers-on were involved. Punch was haunted by a vision of the starving poor, who continually intruded in their rags and distress into so many of the first radical cartoons. It was bad enough for England to be forced to pay Prince Albert a yearly allowance of £30,000, which had only been granted after an acrimonious debate in the House of Commons. But what was the necessity of giving £23,000 a year 'from the sweat of Englishmen' to the Duke of Cumberland, the fifth son of George III, who through the giddy revolutions of the nineteenth-century royal

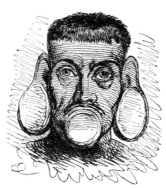

Another favourite theme which continued to feature in Punch throughout the Victorian era was the harmful effects of civilization. Here an ordinary Botecudo (top) is seen after his own and Western culture have done their worst (1841)

merry-go-round had become the King of Hanover in 1837? Another pensioner was Leopold I of the Belgians, the uncle of Queen Victoria, and the widower of the heiress-apparent, Princess Charlotte, who had died in 1817 after giving birth to a still-born child. When both Leopold and the King of Hanover arrived in London for a wedding in 1843, Punch noted that the royal pensioners had arrived at a most appropriate time: a quarter day. The marriage itself did nothing to mollify Punch's wrath, but only served to inflame it, for this union between Princess Augusta and yet another minor German prince would produce only one more pensioner. The Prince of Mecklenburg-Strelitz had come 'not only to take an English wife, but with her, three thousand pounds per annum of English money', which would be used 'to gild the shabby Court of Mecklenburg with new splendour'. In contrast, it was noted, the total amount spent on educating the poor of England, at that time was £10,000 a year. This was the pure, uncorrupted voice of early nineteenth-century radicalism, the fight against 'old corruption' which had thrown up in the previous generation such John-Bullish reformers as William Cobbett.

Many of the great issues of the day were seen in the same morally simplistic light. The middle-class manufacturers, who had gained the vote in 1832, were now demanding a new reform, the repeal of the Corn Laws, which maintained the price of home-grown wheat by putting a duty on imported grain. The manufacturers wanted cheap bread so that they could continue to pay low wages to their workers, and thus make their products more competitive on the world market. As it was, the high price of bread which, with potatoes, was then the staple diet of the masses, benefited scarcely anyone, neither the tenant farmers who found it difficult to sell their high-priced grain and other products in a low-wage economy, nor the farm labourers who were forced to work long hours for starvation wages of seven or nine shillings a week. The only group which really profited was the landed aristocracy, as protection enabled them to maintain their vast estates intact.

Punch was against protection, though it liked neither the man, 'Sir Rhubarb Pill', nor the means by which he eventually forced through the repeal of the Corn Laws in 1846. But it was even more fundamentally opposed to the old nobility, arrogant, parasitical, authoritarian, who had dominated English society for so many centuries. They were continually parodied, censured and reviled. The Duke of Cambridge, the seventh son of George III, was not praised for his public spirit in presiding at so many banquets, but rebuked for his meanness in saving on his own household expenses. In 1843, Punch saw fit to publish an announcement:

IMPORTANT TO SOCIETIES

We regret to state that, in obedience to the strict injunctions of his physicians, the Duke of Cambridge will, in future, not be able to dine at more than six public dinners a week.

The expenses of
A GRATUITOUS VISIT TO BLENHEIM

	s.	d.
The very civil gentleman who shows the keeper's lodge ..	5	0
The gentleman on a fine horse who accompanies parties through the park, giving the names of trees, and remarking that it is a very fine day	5	0
The gentleman who shows the garden	5	0
The gentleman's gentleman who shows the kitchen.........	5	0
The urbane gentleman who takes care of your umbrella, and never takes anything but silver	2	6
The lady who opens the gate	2	6
The noble lady who is condescending enough to describe the pictures as quick as she can, so as to have finished with the stupid business as soon as possible......................	5	0
Incidental expenses to endless little boys and girls, 'pampered menials' etc. etc..	10	0

Total per head (*very cheap*) £2 0 0

The above does not include any gratuity to the DUKE OF MARLBOROUGH

1847

Another enterprising 'showman', the Duke of Marlborough, had already started to open his country estate of Blenheim to the public, and when in 1846 he started to sell game from his estate, it was suggested that 'Licensed to deal in game' might be added to his family crest. A new Order of the Mutton was presented to the Duke of Sutherland who had evicted thousands of tenants from his Scottish estates to make pastures for more profitable sheep. Evictions of tenants by hard-hearted aristocrats always aroused scorn for the evictor and sympathy for the victim. In 1845 the Duke of Buckingham was castigated for turning out the widow of a tenant farmer at Winchendon March, whose family had spent hundreds of pounds on draining and improving the land, which they had farmed for generations. But the greatest vituperation was reserved for the Duke of Norfolk, who had the stupidity to suggest that if the starving poor of England could not afford to buy bread, they should eat curry powder instead.

This fatuous suggestion which was made at the prize fat-stock show at Steyning, Sussex on December 8, 1845, amazed and amused even his local, feudally dominated audience, so that, according to the report in *The Times*, his speech was punctuated by gasps of astonishment and gusts of laughter. The Duke said, 'I don't mean to say it will make a good soup, but this I say, that if a man comes home, and has nothing better, it will make him warm and go to bed comfortable. . . . I don't say it may be given in quantities; but with potatoes, or a little bit of bacon, or anything of that kind, it is like a pickle. . . . I mean to try it among my labourers, and by doing that I am sure that if the winter comes on severe, we may add very much to the comforts of the poor.' This piece of truly Christian solicitude for the poor provided Punch with a happy Christmas and a Merry New Year: humorous variations on the original humourless theme were played for many weeks afterwards. When it was discovered that the Duke's second title was the Earl of Surrey, Punch announced with respectful solemnity that 'the present head of the illustrious race intends to change Surrey into Curry'. A collection of mock testimonials from grateful beneficiaries was also published.

TESTIMONIALS
FOR THE DUKE OF NORFOLK'S CURRY

SIR,—I have been for years subject to apoplectic attacks. A friend recommended me to try your celebrated curry powder. I persevered, against considerable nausea, for ten days, and I am so reduced now, that my medical man assures me that I shall never have another fit of apoplexy as long as I live.

I remain, Sir,
Your altered Servant,
ANTHONY GAWGE.

BENEVOLENT SIR,—I have thirty little boys entrusted to my matronly care; and, wishing to add to their comfort, I have given them, every morning and evening, a large mixture, compounded of the materials so kindly suggested to you by a lady, for whom I shall always feel the greatest gratitude. The boys like it much better than the milk-and-water they used to have before; but I am sure they cannot be so grateful to you for the suggestion as their affectionate mother and mistress,

DEBORAH BIRCH.

Dove's Nest,
Preparatory School for little boys from 3 to 20.

SIR,—I like your curry very much. I tried it yesterday with a rabbit, and it is astonishing how it improved it. It was exceedingly warm and comfortable.

Hoping you will believe me,
I remain, worthy Sir,
Your obedient Servant,
EBENEZER FOGUEY.

P.S. You may make any use you like of this.

HONOURABLE SIR,—I was at a loss to know how I could reduce the expenses of the workhouse of which I am the Master. Your recommendation, however, has helped me out of the difficulty. I have prescribed it in all manner of ways, both in hot and cold water, and can safely say it goes a very great way. I give each pauper a pinch, and I never knew the instance of one asking for more.

Every workhouse in the kingdom and every pauper in it should thank you, Sir. At all events, you may depend on the gratitude of

Your obedient Servant,
THOS. FLINT HARDY.

I expect to save 40*l.* a year by it.

SIR,—Two months ago,—*i. e.* before the Panic,—I was a Railway Director, with a fund of 2,000,000*l.* at my disposal—on paper. I was then luxuriating on all the delicacies of the season, from Champagne to Carrara water; but now I am living on your inestimable curry. You cannot imagine, with plenty of boiling water, how warm it is; and I am sure it must be very healthy, because I always leave off eating it with an appetite. Besides, I am no longer subjected to the dreadful headaches I invariably had after eating and drinking in the days of my credit and prosperity. Another recommendation for your curry is, that a little of it is as good as a feast. One pinch always satisfies me.

Yours, anything you like,
REGINALD PENTONVILLE.

Whitecross Prison.
Please send me fifty boxes.

GENEROUS SIR,—You will mightily oblige me by sending me a ship-load of your beautiful curry. I wish to distribute it to my tenantry at this time of the year, when famine and disease are running over the country like a regiment of Saxon soldiers, killing everybody they meet. I cannot bear to see my poor tenants crying for food over an empty pot, as long as I have the means to buy them something to put into it, which will make their hearts warm and comfortable. Sure a few pinches of curry will not be the less welcome to them because they are offered by the liberal hand of their Regenerator and Liberator,

DANIEL O'CONNELL.

Direct them to *Derrynane Beg*. There are hundreds who will bless the day they get it!

1846

As a class, politicians, both Whig and Tory, were almost equally anathema. With a few exceptions, such as Joseph Hume, the radical member for Montrose, they were depicted as self-seeking, time-serving humbugs. An article in the very first volume, 'Hints to New Members', by An Old Trimmer, proclaimed that it was already 'an established axiom that every member goes into Parliament for the sole purpose of advancing his own private interest and not, as has been ignorantly believed, for the benefit of his country or the constituency he represents'. A few members were singled out for unending abuse: Sir Robert Peel for his deviousness; Lord Brougham for his arrogance and vanity; Disraeli for his ambitious assertiveness; Daniel O'Connell, the Irish Liberator, for his constant agitation for repeal of the union; and Colonel Sibthorp, MP for Lincoln (immortalized only through these attacks), for his reactionary views about almost everything.

Practically all branches of the establishment—MPs, lords, business men, manufacturers, bankers, lawyers, clergymen— became involved in the railway mania of the 1840s, the biggest financial speculation in England since the South Sea Bubble of the eighteenth century. Financiers and other gamblers made thousands of pounds by floating fraudulent companies and speculating in railway shares, which were bought and sold as carelessly as a quarter of a pound of tea. The amalgamation of scattered lines into composite networks, serving a whole area of the country, enabled speculators such as George Hudson, the 'Railway King' to make immense fortunes. 'Although England will never be in chains,' Punch commented, in 1845, 'she will pretty soon be in irons, as a glance at the numerous new railway prospectuses will testify.' Three fourths of the advertised schemes were 'arrant bubbles' and a similar proportion of the shareholders were 'men of straw'. One new company, the Somersetshire and North Devon Junction, which claimed to have a capital of £600,000, proposed to build a line to connect places 'into which the wildest fancy and the most errant donkey never travelled'. The new railway line would allow militia-men to be transported from other parts of the country to protect that stretch of coastline, which had previously been invaded by Hubba, the Dane, in the time of Alfred the Great!

To attract reputable sponsors, 'King' Hudson gave away thousands of shares in his numerous companies to members of the old nobility, a few of whom had the honesty to return them to the companies after Hudson's downfall in 1849. Railway lines could be built only after a private Bill had been passed in parliament and Punch commented, mildly for once, that 'we don't like to see Members of Parliament dabbling in railway speculations, which they themselves have the opportunity of unduly favouring in the House of Commons'. There were rich pickings, too, for lawyers: it was estimated in 1844 that they stood to gain £100,000 in all by

---

PERSONALITIES OF THE YEAR

Delightful Novelty

We are charmed to see in the shops a new portrait of PRINCE ALBERT. It is very much wanted; and makes, we think, the forty-fifth this year.

A Hint to the Lords

There has been a deal of talk in the House of Commons about some new marine glue, which is so adhesive, that when two things have been joined together by it, it is impossible to separate them. If it were made into lip-salve, what a friendly present it would be to LORD BROUGHAM.

Highly Appropriate

Ireland, we understand, at the dictation of DANIEL O'CONNELL, is about to repudiate the shamrock, and instead of it to assume, for a national emblem, the aspen, as typical of eternal agitation.

Despotism in Russia

The EMPEROR OF RUSSIA has banished into Siberia a Professor of the University of Moscow, because he had published a book with the title of 'The *Revolution* of the Stars'.

1845

representing railway companies at committee hearings in the House.

As in all speculative booms, the interests of the customers were sacrificed to quick profits. Punch launched a campaign for safer and more comfortable railways which it maintained for many years. The inclusion of so many clergymen on the boards of 'bubble' companies made Punch suggest that one parson might be spared to travel with each train 'to administer consolation in the case of a mortal casualty'. The provision of padded suits for passengers was proposed as another panacea and all passengers were advised to include in their luggage for these perilous journeys a copy of the Railway Pocket Companion, a finely bound compendium, containing 'a small bottle of water, a tumbler, a

---

SHEEP IN RAILWAY TRAINS

What a wonderful improvement has taken place in the temper of the British Public! To such a proficiency have they attained in the virtue of patience, that they will now not only put up with any injustice or imposition, but submit to be treated with the greatest contempt and insolence into the bargain. They are content to travel in railway pens, like sheep to the slaughter, injured, deluded, derided, and only bleating in return. . . .

Ah! there was a time, very considerably within the memory of man, when this public, so tame now, could not be put upon at so little expense. If merely swindled by a playhouse manager, it would deface ornaments and tear up benches. What would have happened, in those days, if free-born British passengers had been systematically delayed, endangered, and moreover mocked and set at nought, by boards of unscrupulous, avaricious, dividend-grasping, screwing, bloated railway directors? But now, as the public no longer takes the law into its own hands, and does mischief, it ought to insist upon legal damages in the event of accident or stoppage.

1852

RAILWAY MAXIMS

(Perfectly at the Service of any Railway Company)

Delays are dangerous.
A Train in time saves nine.
Live and let live.
Between two Trains we fall to the ground.
A Director is known by the Company he keeps.
A Railway Train is the Thief of Time.
There is no place like Home—but the difficulty is to get there.
The farther you go, the worse is your fare.
It's the Railway pace that kills.
A Railway is long, but Life is short—and generally the longer a railway, the shorter your life.

1853

The Momentous Question: 'Tell me, oh tell me, dearest Albert, have *you* any railway shares?' (1845)

complete set of surgical instruments, a packet of lint, and directions for making a will'.

The electric telegraph was patented by Sir William Wheatstone and Sir William Fothergill Cooke in 1837, and was adopted by the Great Western Railway in the following year. The telegraph had many different uses. It enabled a uniform, or 'railway time' as it was then called to be introduced throughout the country; it proved useful on several occasions for the apprehension of criminals, including one suspected murderer who had boarded a train at

'Capital and Labour' (1843)

A RAILWAY COMPANY'S QUESTION

(Chairman sings)

Again there's one collision more!
  Lots killed and maimed; I say,
My Colleagues, what an awful bore!
  There will be much to pay.

The damages for limbs and lives
  Will heavy prove, dear friends,
And, howsoever business thrives,
  Reduce our dividends.

An Actuary should compute
  What loss from year to year,
We from those accidents, the fruit
  Of overwork, may fear.

Whether 'twere cheaper in the end,
  Those frequent fines to bear.
Or cash enough in wages spend
  To make collision rare?

We want more skilled hands; there's no doubt;
  Each pointsman no mere clown:
How little could we give without
  Our having them break down?

1872

Slough and was arrested on his arrival in London; and it helped to increase safety by improving communications between stations. Punch made great fun of the electric telegraph, failing to see that it could provide a means of combating the rail accidents which it so greatly deplored. It was not until 1870 that the Midland Railway introduced a system of 'block' signalling by telegraph for whole sections of the track, which allowed trains to be kept at a safe distance from each other. Punch welcomed this innovation, preferring it to the 'blockhead' system, which had previously prevailed, but the 'block' system was not made compulsory by law

STEAM-BOAT STATISTICS

We find by statistical returns that there are about thirty steam-boats running between London Bridge and Richmond, all of which have at different times run against the tide, while twenty-five have had the benefit of the wind on some occasions. Sixteen have run aground, and twelve have run into fourteen, while the remaining six have dashed against the bridges. Out of thirty Captains, two have served in the Royal Navy as cabin-boys, sixteen have been in the Merchant Service as barge-men, and all have rowed wherries between London and Westminster.

1842

for all railways until 1889! Safety in transport is often given a much lower priority than speed and profits.

The discomfort, delays and discourtesies of rail travel provoked as much irritation as they do today. Many columns were devoted to middle-class complaints about lazy booking clerks, lack of facilities and lost luggage. The whole of the Almanack for 1846 was devoted to Railway Miseries: the fisherman, for example, who had travelled out to Maidenhead for a quiet day's sport and was presented on arrival with a box of glass, and a parrot in a cage, by a porter who informed him that, unfortunately, his fishing rod and live bait had been sent on to Bristol.

But the main sympathy was reserved for the poor, third-class passenger. To encourage more people to travel by train, parliament passed a Railways Act in 1844 which made it compulsory for all companies to run at least one train a day on all of their lines at a fare of a penny a mile. Many railway companies evaded the spirit of the law by running just one 'parliamentary train' in the middle of the night at the minimum legally-permitted speed of 12 mph. Third-class passengers who travelled in open carriages, like cattle trucks, could be exposed to rain, sleet, wind or snow for twenty-four hours on a journey which was done by first-class trains in a quarter of the time. Or, if they were thoughtless enough to get up from their wooden seats without looking, they might have their heads knocked off, literally, by a particularly low bridge. They had to wait until 1874 before one of the more enterprising companies, the Midland, abolished the second-class and allowed third-class passengers to travel in comfortable, closed second-class carriages without any increase in fares.

Travellers by excursion trains fared little better. The first cheap excursion by train had been organized in 1841 by Thomas Cook, the founder of the great travel and tourist agency, for Leicester teetotallers to attend a temperance meeting in nearby Lough-borough. Excursions soon became popular with artisans who wanted to give their families a cheap day out at the seaside, but the

---

A NEW MILKY WAY

Kirchoff, a Prussian chemist, is reported to have discovered a process by which milk may be preserved for an indefinite period. Fresh milk is evaporated by a gentle heat till it is reduced to a dry powder, which is to be kept perfectly dry in a bottle. When required for use it need only be diluted with a sufficient quantity of water. Mr. James Jones, who keeps a red cow—over his door—claims the original idea of making milk from a white powder, which, he states, may be done without the tedious process of evaporation, by using an article entirely known to London milk-vendors—namely *chalk*.

1841

trains were slow and the service was often sketchy: it was noted for Whit Monday, 1845, that it was 'sufficient for an individual to announce that he had got an Excursion Ticket to make him at once a subject of total neglect from clerks, porters, and indeed from all railway authorities'.

The bursting of the railway bubble in the following year brought no tears to Mr Punch's eyes. He gloated over the downfall of 'King' Hudson and the rumoured flight of several city aldermen to far-off asylums on the Continent, and gleefully portrayed railway surveyors pawning their theodolites and former railway directors begging for a coin from passing ladies in their new employment of road-crossing sweeper. His compassion did not extend to failed speculators or profiteers, who were to remain just as reprehensible to the mature, respectable Mr Punch during the Boer War as they had been in his radical beginnings; but it was reserved for those who had been made poor by the exploitation of others and for the victims of hypocrisy, humbug, and bumbledom, the unfeeling authorities and the heartless bureaucrats.

A whole generation of the ragged poor, the exploited and the starving stumble and stagger aimlessly through the pages of the early volumes: farm labourers who could not feed their families on their miserable pittance of a few shillings a week; men, women and children who worked long hours in mine, factory and sweat-shop until they were fit to drop, so that others could live in luxury on the products of their unceasing labour. The ill-treatment of paupers, the exploitation of governesses, and the great contrast between

---

MAN *VERSUS* MACHINE

Machinery, in its progress, has doubtless been the origin of terrible calamity; it has made the strong man so much live lumber. But as we cannot go back, and must go on, it is for statesmen and philosophers to prepare for the crisis as surely coming as the morning light. How, when machinery is multiplied—as it will be—a thousandfold? How, when tens of thousand-thousand hands are made idle by the ingenuity of the human mind? How, when, comparatively speaking, there shall be *no* labour for man? Will the multitude lie down and, unrepining, die? We think not—we are sure not. Then will rise—and already we hear the murmur—a cry, a shout for an adjustment of interests; a shout that, hard as it is, will strike upon the heart of Mammon, and make the spoiler tremble.

We put this question to Sir Robert PEEL: if all labour done by man were suddenly performed by machine power, and that power in the possession of some thousand individuals,—what would be the cry of the rest of the race? Would not the shout be—'Share, share'?

The steam engine, despite of themselves, must and will carry statesmen back to first principles. As it is, machinery is a fiend to the poor; the time will come when it will be as a beneficent angel.

1842

'Bubbles of the Year—Cheap Clothing.' Punch was one of the most persistent critics of sweated labour in the rag trade (1845)

the elaborate finery worn by Victorian ladies and the sweated means by which it was produced, were all themes to which Punch returned continually for many years, long after the main radical phase was past, which is both a testament to the durability of Punch's compassion and to the immutability of English society. Thomas Hood's poem, 'The Song of the Shirt', published in 1843, was inspired by the case of a real-life widow with two children who earned the grand total of seven shillings a week by making trousers for which she earned sevenpence a pair:

> O men, with sisters dear!
> O men, with mothers and wives!
> It is not linen you're wearing out,
> But human creatures' lives!
> Stitch—stitch—stitch
> In poverty, hunger and dirt,
> Sewing at once, with a double thread,
> A shroud as well as a shirt.

Although in his constant mockery of emancipated women, Mr Punch might justly be considered as the archetypal 'male chauvinist pig', he consistently protested against the exploitation of educated women, daughters of poor parsons and distressed gentlefolk, who were forced to seek employment as governesses when, in return for their skilled instruction in English, music, French, dancing and art, they could expect to receive, as the numerous advertisements republished from other newspapers testified, the munificent salary of £8 to £20 a year. Even maidservants, who were later to be vilified for their indolence, ignorance and impertinence, were pitied in the early years: in fact, Punch alone of all the nineteenth-century crusaders, pointed an ironic finger of scorn in 1844 at those liberal-minded reformers who exposed the exploitation of women in mine and factory and yet neglected the equal exploitation of 'The White Slave' in their own home.

It's scrub, scrub, scrub from Monday morn, right on to Friday night,
Scrub, scrub, as soon as daylight breaks—scrub, scrub by candlelight.

But only a few months later, Punch, with its incipient change of views, expressed a very different attitude to servants in 'Maxims for Cooks'.

MAXIMS FOR COOKS

1. Keep yourself clean and tidy if you can. If your fingers are greasy, wipe them on your hair, which thus acquires a polish.
2. When a joint comes down from dinner, cut off what you intend for your supper. If cut while the joint is warm, it does not show that it has been cut.
3. If you want a jelly bag, cut up an ironing blanket for the purpose. The former is of course wanted in a hurry, but the latter may be procured at leisure.
4. When your dishes come down stairs, throw them all in scalding water at once. Those that are not broken by the operation may afterwards be taken out, and put in their proper places.
5. Scour your pickle-jars, but empty them first, if you are fond of pickle.
6. If you have been peeling onions, cut bread-and-butter with the same knife; it will show the multifariousness of your occupations, and perhaps give a hint for raising your wages.
7. Let your spit and your skewers be always rusty; or, at least, do not take the trouble to polish them; for by leaving great black holes in the meat, they show it has been roasted, which is always better than being baked, and it will be the more relished in consequence.
8. Never do anything by halves, except lamb, which you must sometimes do by quarters.

1845

TIME *VERSUS* CRIME

At last a mode has been hit upon to lessen what has hitherto been called 'a fearful increase of crime': it is to try all prisoners 'after dinner' (that is, after the Common Serjeant has dined), at the Old Bailey. A few days since, a man was placed at the bar charged with stealing some shovels. The indictment was read, witnesses examined, sentence passed, and the culprit changed into a transport 'for seven years' and all in the short space of something less than *four minutes!* Now, if four minutes will suffice for culprits deserving seven years, eight, will, of course, suffice for fourteen, sixteen for twenty-eight and let us say a whole half-hour, where the sentence is for life.

1843

Above left: The 'speculative mama' was a figure of terror for eligible bachelors at society balls (1842)

Above right: Dancing could be one of the great social miseries for the inexpert (1842)

Sympathy was also extended in the early years to all victims of officialdom, whether it was private—the flunkeys, footmen and beadles in their gold lace, the 'foolish frippery of bygone ages'—or public—the hard-hearted workhouse officials and the unsympathetic magistrates and judges of the courts. When workers in their fustian jackets were prevented by the keepers from entering St James's Park, which was then reserved for the privileged and the respectable classes, its comment was: 'In merry England, labour is ignominy. Your only man is the man with white hands and filbert nails.' Attention was repeatedly drawn to the unfairness of English courts, where the sentence was often decided by the cut of the accused man's clothes. When a poor countryman was imprisoned for ten weeks after failing to pay a shilling fine and fourteen shillings costs for not attending church one Sunday, it was suggested that the police 'should be empowered to seize upon all suspected non-churchgoers every Saturday night, keeping them in the station houses until Sunday morning, and then marching them, securely handcuffed, up the middle aisle of the parish church.' This system, plus a little private whipping in the vestry for persistent offenders, would provide an even better demonstration of Christian conduct. Constant protests were made against excessively quick trials, vicious sentences, the cutting of offenders' hair in prison and in court, and the hideous spectacle of public hangings, which delighted only the mob, and fashionable ladies and gentlemen who would pay up to £15 for a window-seat in one of the houses facing Newgate gaol in London. Public executions were not abolished until 1868, when some other

'The game laws, or the sacrifice of
the peasant to the hare' (1844)

European countries had already ended capital punishment altogether.

Death or imprisonment, however, were often preferable in those grim times to incarceration in one of the huge, heartless workhouses which had been built all over England after the passing of the Poor Law Amendment Act of 1834, some of which still remain to serve us as National Health hospitals. To discourage the 'idle poor', or what we should now call 'social security scroungers', life in the workhouse was made even harder than that experienced by the poorest labourer outside. Husbands and wives were strictly segregated so that they could not breed any more children who might become a burden on the poor rate. (It was not until 1885 that even those couples who were too old to produce any more children were allowed to live together.) Children were also snatched from their mother's breast and brought to them during the day only to be fed.

One of the most pathetic stories concerned John Matthews, who had left his wife and children in a workhouse while he walked to Wales to seek, unsuccessfully, for work. On his return he was imprisoned for two months in Brinkworth gaol, in Wiltshire, for failing to maintain his family. He was discharged in bitter, freezing weather, having exchanged the warm, woollen prison clothes for his pauper's garb of an old waistcoat and a thin slop, and, with nowhere else to go, stayed in a roadside hovel for four days with nothing to eat but a hunk of bread, which the authorities had generously donated at the prison gate. He died of frostbite, and a weak—or broken—heart.

In those early, grim days of the reign—the era of Disraeli's 'two nations', the rich and the poor—the red blood of radicalism pulsed strongly in Mr Punch's veins. He was opposed to all forms of brutality, whether it originated in the workhouse, on the duelling field, or on the quarter-deck. With the evangelists of Exeter Hall, whom he otherwise execrated, Mr Punch preached incessantly against duelling, even when, as in 1843, such distinguished combatants as the Duke of Wellington and the Earl of Winchilsea were involved. The senseless laws of honour among officers and gentlemen left many wives bereaved and penniless.

He was equally opposed to the use of the whip and scourge, whether it was wielded by some foreign tyrant or by a non-commissioned officer in the Forces. Like an earlier reformer, William Cobbett, who had been imprisoned for two years in 1810 for denouncing the flogging of soldiers, Douglas Jerrold had seen this brutal punishment for himself when he served as a midshipman in the Navy. The 'flowing streamers' in the caps of Her Majesty's Regiments of Foot became symbolic of the cat 'the nine hard cords, about twenty-one inches long, each cord having nine knots', which tore into the soldier's back 'like the talons of a hawk'. A cartoon in 1846 showed two effete officers in mufti, surrounded by decanters and pet dogs, with one saying to the

In its early radical days, Punch published many cartoons illustrating its pity for the poor. Above left: 'The Poor man's friend' (1845) and (above right) 'The Milk of Poor-Law Kindness' (1843)

other: 'What d—— nawnsense it is of a parcel of people talking about doing away with flogging in the Army! I should just like to know what's to be done with a man who dwinks.'

Soldiers had to live on semi-starvation wages, as they still had to do during the Crimean War, and sailors who had been press-ganged or who had volunteered, were discharged without a penny piece of compensation, or pension, when their services were no

---

OUR NATIONAL DEFENCES

It is extremely gratifying to have had the assurance of Ministers, that in the event of war requiring the whole of our troops, England has still got the Chelsea pensioners to fall back upon. The wooden walls of England are safe while she has still her wooden legs to stand upon.

We understand that a review of the Chelsea pensioners will shortly take place, as a preliminary to bringing the veterans into active service. There may be some difficulty in obeying the words of command, for the ordinary operation of shouldering arms will be somewhat of a puzzle to those who have no arms to shoulder. 'Recover arms' will be an evolution that many would be delighted to perform if it were practicable, and 'Stand at ease' will be a suggestion that those who have lost their legs may find some difficulty in complying with.

1845

longer required. The streets of London were full of ill or wounded sailors who were forced to beg for a living: one of the best-known Poor Jacks carried his two-year-old daughter in a Punch-and-Judy style box strapped to his back.

The working classes did not accept their fate without protest. The earlier struggle for the first Reform Bill had brought the country nearer to civil war than it had ever been since Cromwell's days, though his armed uprising had also, despite all its initial democratic hopes, produced nothing in the end but a victory for a new establishment. When working-class hopes were disappointed in 1832, they continued with their struggle for parliamentary reform: one man, one vote; a secret ballot; annual elections; equal electoral districts; payment of MPs and the abolition of the property qualification. With the support of some middle-class Midlands reformers, the Chartists organized a nationwide petition for reform which weighed 6 cwt and which had been signed by 1.25 million people. It was presented to the House of Commons on July 12, 1839, but was rejected. There were calls for a general strike, and disturbances in many different parts of the country, the biggest in Newport, Monmouthshire, where troops opened fire, killing twenty-four Chartists and wounding forty others. Many Chartist leaders were arrested and transported. In spite of this, agitation still continued. A second, even larger petition was presented to Parliament in 1842 and the third, and final petition in 1848.

Punch had no time for female Chartists or for agitators who did nothing but 'flatter the mob' and hire 'bagmen' with good lungs to travel around the countryside shouting their praises; but it did support the genuine Chartists, whose movement had been born out of 'defeated hopes' over the Reform Bill. 'The vice of the age,' it wrote in 1842, 'is a want of sympathy with the condition of the great mass of people. They are looked upon as the mere instruments of wealth.' There were some 'hard-hearted logicians' among the Chartists, who were demanding nothing but the 'inalienable rights of humanity'.

Support for the working classes as a whole was to be quickly eroded, but one characteristic attitude which never faltered from first to last, was Punch's patriotism. However much it criticized English humbug, corruption or incompetence itself, it would never brook any foreign criticism or threats from any corner of the world. 'Punch', it was baldly stated in 1846, 'is proud of his country.' It strongly opposed the agitation for the repeal of the Act of Union of 1800 which had made the whole of Ireland subject to direct rule from Westminster; and there was little sympathy for the Irish even during the terrible potato famine of 1845–49. Page after page was peppered with savage verbal and pictorial attacks on Daniel O'Connell who led the fight for repeal. Many other arch enemies were forgiven immediately after they had died. Peel's death, for example, was commemorated in Punch by a memorial stone composed of loaves of cheap bread; but the anti-Irish feeling

Opposite: Poor Jack (1841)

Above right: John Leech's view of a female Chartist (1842)

A WORD OF ADVICE

What can be done with Ireland? Kindness, judging from the speeches of Young Ireland, is thrown away upon her. Every sympathy is shown to her distress, that charity can devise and money execute; but it all goes for nothing. She rejects the sympathy, and only keeps the money. Instead of saying 'Thank you' she does nothing but heap abuses on the hand that relieves her. We wonder what will satisfy Ireland?

A New Cry

It is curious that the Irish still cry out for Repeal, and yet they are rushing over to England in thousands every day. We begin to imagine this cry of 'Repeal' is directed against Ireland, considering the alacrity the 'finest peasantry' show in leaving it. It cannot be against England, or else they would never seek food and shelter in the very country they so bitterly denounce. The best thing for Ireland will be a poor law, with workhouses established all through the kingdom, on a kindly, charitable plan, making the landlords contribute largely to their support. The best cry for this purpose will be 'Union'.

1847

was so strong in England that attacks on O'Connell continued for many years after his death, which occurred in 1847 while he was on a journey to Rome. It was not until 1869, twenty-two years later, when his remains were brought back to be buried in Glasnevin cemetery, Dublin, that he was ultimately pardoned, almost:

> There's time to be gen'rous, nor narrowly scan
> The stains on a mem'ry, the faults in a man....
> Let us think of the warm heart, still open, at need,
> To the wronged of his race, the oppressed of his creed....

Many foreign rulers were condemned as tyrants in their own country, or as threats to the British balance of power which preserved world peace, sometimes for both reasons. The Napoleonic wars and colonial rivalries had made England deeply suspicious of France. Punch loved the country's rulers no more than its milliners. In 1843, the magazine was banned from France for a time for its personal attacks on the king, Louis-Philippe, and his aggressive colonial policy in Algeria—'the born right of every Frenchman to carry fire and bloodshed into every country he can get into'. Nicholas I, Tsar of Russia, was denounced as a despot and a tyrant for the rape of Poland in 1830–31 and the alleged flogging of some nuns at Minsk. As we have already seen, Punch was no

Daniel O'Connell, the Irish politician, who was seen as 'the real potato blight of Ireland' (1845)

Above left: 'Young Ireland in business for himself.' Young Ireland, a revolutionary movement, was also attacked bitterly in cartoons and words (1846)

Above right: In a rare moment of sympathy for the Irish, Punch shows a youthful Queen Victoria conceding to the Tsar, Nicholas I, that they were wrong in their treatment of Ireland and Poland respectively (1844)

lover of the Germans. The new Prussian constitution of 1846 was welcomed because it would reduce the size of the police force to only three million; prohibit Prussians from serving in the army if they were less than ten and more than fifty years of age; and encourage the whole nation to joke indiscriminately 'to the fullest extent a German is capable of'.

JONATHANISMS

A house-painter in New York grained a door so exactly in imitation of oak, that last year it put forth a quantity of leaves, and grew an excellent crop of acorns.

A correspondent of a Picayune paper has such a cold in his head, that he can't wash his face without freezing the water.

There's an old fellow in Nashville who snores so loud, that he is obliged to sleep at a house in the next street, to avoid awakening himself.

1842

No special relationship with America flourished at that time. The Americans were regularly condemned for their slavery, their lynch law, their repudiation of foreign debts, and their liking for hand pistols and the whip. Relations between the two countries were also soured by the protracted negotiations over the boundary

ENGLAND

AMERICA

between Canada and the United States—the Oregon dispute. When there was some war talk in the United States in 1846, Punch reported sarcastically: 'The American government must be in earnest about the Oregon question, for we have just heard that General Tom Thumb has received an order to return immediately to his country to take over the command of the Yankee Army.' Punch, like many of its middle-class readers, had a simple answer to all questions of foreign policy, from which it scarcely ever deviated: my country, right or wrong.

THE YANKEE BOATSWAIN'S SONG

To the American Slave-Navy

Heave away, my tight niggers, my jolly brisk blacks—
Ain't there Tar in your very complexion?—
Here's a hearty good lash, boys, around, for your backs,
You'll be smarter, I guess, for correction.
To your swabs and your Britishers patter, d'ye see,
Of Oppression and Wrong and all that,
Where's the true Yankee nigger who'd wish to be free,
Or would make a wry face at the Cat?

Don't you serve a Republic that's glorious and great?
Don't it flog universal creation?
Ain't you walloped, you dogs, for the good of the State—
The enlighten'd American nation?
Go-ahead then, like lightning, my sooty-faced tars,
With 'Yoho' at the top of your pipes;
Stick like Wax to your colours, the stripes and the stars,
And give thanks to your stars for your stripes.

1844

SPECIMEN OF A NEW ANGLO-INDIAN DICTIONARY

Cowardice. Any one striking you when your hands are held.
Fair play. Yourself striking another person whilst his hands are held.
Keranie. A helot, or clerk, in a government office, who is retained because he is indispensable, and is consequently detested.
Gentleness. Any 'gentleman' knocking down a 'nigger', and then kicking him for falling.
Cruelty. A plebeian presuming to chastise his 'nigger'.
Witness, Native. A man hired for a few pence to perjure himself by the hour.

1844

Opposite: 'What? You young yankee-noodle, strike your own father!' (1846)

2 THE RISING GENERATION

1847–1851

By 1851—the year of the Great Exhibition—Punch had changed; its readers had changed; England, itself, had changed significantly. Many of the contributors who had given Punch its radical attitudes had departed. Thomas Hood had died in 1845; Henry Mayhew had finally severed his connections with the magazine in the same year; and Douglas Jerrold who, above all, had been responsible for the initial tone, was contributing less and less after 1848. It is somewhat doubtful if their old-style radicalism had ever appealed greatly to the majority of the readers, who desired to be amused rather than instructed, as was demonstrated by the phenomenal success of the first Almanack, with its multitude of jokes, which sent the circulation bounding up from six thousand to ninety thousand for that issue.

The original readers had also changed. Adolescents had become mature men who no longer trailed radical clouds of glory from their youth: they were by then established in their careers and involved in their domestic life and their growing number of children, who appeared with the frequency of rabbits in Victorian times. Some of them- had doubtless become successful and prosperous, the kind of portly, well-dressed man of early middle-age who appears so commonly in the cartoons of the late 1840s. There is nothing that makes men—and women —forget their earlier beliefs more quickly than climbing a rung or two up the social ladder, an ascent which could be made most quickly in those days of unbounded business opportunity, when income tax was still only three per cent. Even any surviving radicals among them must by then have become far more concerned with preserving the peace between their wives and their maids (and sometimes themselves), than with establishing a wider social harmony—as such a development is an almost inevitable result of increasing maturity.

Punch did not shake off its radicalism immediately. 'It is our duty,' it wrote in 1847, 'to smash humbug of every description.' There were still some attacks on the landed aristocrats, who were generally advised in the same year that they could make far better use of their estates by indulging in the more rational 'sport' of peasant-preserving rather than pheasant-preserving. The Earl of Harewood was ticked off for prohibiting farm workers on his northern estates from taking in lodgers or allowing their married children to live at home without permission. If there was

---

A NEW SERVANTS' OFFICE

The following questions have been drawn up, which must be satisfactorily answered by those masters and mistresses who are desirous of securing the benefit of domestic assistance:

1. Do you allow beer-money, and an unlimited supply of milk, so that the former may be saved by the drinking of the latter?
2. When you give out sugar for puddings or pies, are you particular to a pound or two?
3. When you have a joint at table, do you ever expect to see it again under any circumstances whatever?
4. How many cousins do you allow each servant to have in the division of police that does duty in your neighbourhood?
5. Do you consider 'He is my cousin' a sufficient explanation of any man being found on your premises at any hour?
6. Are you prepared to give a character half a dozen times over, in the event of your situation, and five more after yours, being found unsuitable?

1847

---

overcrowding on the estate, the Earl was advised to build more cottages; and if he wanted to stop 'improvident marriages' he could always pay higher wages instead. Attacks were also made on the annuity of £12,000 granted to the Duke of Cambridge at a time when government clerks (some of whom were possibly Punch readers) were threatened with a cut in their salaries. In the following year, some officers of the 15th Hussars and the 16th Lancers, who had pelted civilians with rotten eggs on their return from the Epsom races, were condemned for their 'disgraceful' behaviour, which would add 'another achievement to the brilliant onslaughts of the British Army'. Their 'eggs-emplary' conduct in not turning up in court next day, after they had promised to do so, would bring further honour to the title of 'officer and gentleman'. The Ecclesiastical Commissioners were also strongly criticized for their 'midsummer madness' in spending £128,320 on building and refurbishing the palaces of six bishops, at a time when 'poor incumbents' (many of whom were Punch readers) lived in ruined parsonages which they were forced to repair at their own expense. William Calcraft, the public hangman from 1828 to 1874, remained as odious as ever. When he was summoned for failing to support his mother, Punch gleefully asked the supporters of the final deterrent why 'the great teacher himself, should bring away such low morality from the great public school, the scaffold?' It was noted that the hearing of the case was attended by a number of well-dressed ladies. All Punch's indignant horror was aroused when Charlotte Harris of Taunton, Somerset, who had been found guilty of poisoning her husband, was told that she would have to wait until her baby was born before the execution was carried out. Punch also composed a valedictory salutation for the Poor Law

Previous page: A group of workmen having a break during the reassembling of the Crystal Palace at Sydenham, after it was moved from Hyde Park in 1854

Commissioners, who were replaced by a new Board responsible to a Minister after the Andover workhouse scandal:

> Farewell; good friends, if I may call
> One man among you friend,
> Assembled to behold our fall,
> And view our shameful end. . . .

These, however, were mainly legacies of the radical past. Between 1846 and 1847 there was a distinct change of style (manifested earlier in the cartoons rather than in the text), as Mark Lemon, who was by then in sole charge, increasingly imposed his own surer grasp of the readers' attitudes, and prejudices, upon the magazine—an essential element of any great editor—making it far more like the Victorian Punch we all know. Radicalism became unfashionable in England after 1848, the year of the revolutions on the Continent, which also saw the publication of the *Communist Manifesto* by Marx and Engels. England remained secure, its capital ringed by troops, under the command of the Duke of Wellington, to prevent any trouble during the presentation of the third, and final, Chartist petition. Faced with the threat of armed confrontation, the Chartist leader, Feargus O'Connor, called off the planned march on parliament and presented the petition without the support of a procession of his supporters. The petition

'The Kings in their cock-boats.' The 1848 revolutions brought trouble to many crowned heads of Europe, but not to the British queen (1848)

was said to contain over five million signatures—about one fifth of the total population of Britain then—but middle-class fears about the growth of radical feeling turned to mocking laughter when it was discovered that it bore less than two million signatures, many of them duplicates; others, forgeries; and some, ironic, such as 'Queen Victoria' and 'the Duke of Wellington', contributed, perhaps, by Punch readers, who knows? Punch celebrated the country's escape from anarchy and violence by publishing a double-page cartoon early in 1849, showing a contented English-man, his wife and their nine children, sitting in domestic bliss at home, while all around them the continental guns roared and the mobs shouted. The title, an epitome of the Victorian age, was 'There is no Place like Home'.

In Punch, the ends change more quickly than the means. Although it expressed some sympathy with the demands of draper's assistants for the earlier closing of their shops, which did not then shut until nine or ten at night, it dismissed as a piece of 'foolery' their plans to open a model establishment, where they could be their own masters at the expense of the great British public, who were being asked to subscribe £150,000 in £10 shares. There was no sympathy either for the socialistic dawn, the ultimate aim and intention of Chartism, which it had once supported. Marx and Engels made less impact in England then, and aroused fewer fears, than the dangerous radicals and anarchists of France, 'Pierre Leroux, Considerat, Proudhon & Cie', as they were styled, whose socialism was 'a constant round of abuse'. Readers were assured that their system of 'share and share alike' was only a cloak for all sorts of robberies; when hundreds combined to throw everything they had into 'one pot', you could be sure that nothing would ever be seen again, except by the two or three appointed to keep the pot boiling. The real turning point in Punch's affections came in 1849. Beggars, like Poor Jack, were no longer depicted as hallowed innocents and sufferers. The 'begging profession', for that is what it had by then become, had been infiltrated by a new breed of 'actors of misery' who practised many 'infamous tricks' to divert alms from the deserving poor. Even charity had been put in a straitjacket of suspicion.

Punch turned increasingly to other, more amusing, things. It had always kept a watchful eye on the foibles of social and domestic life remember the Speculative Mamma—in its own parish of the great city of London. These topics were to become far more predominant in the years that followed. Although there was still no place like home, the pleasures of domestic life were not unmixed with pains and penalties, such as awful children, the 'rising generation', nagging wives, impudent maids, dinners of cold mutton, bills, and expensive household repairs. Punch did not admire mothers who indulged in baby talk—'tootsey-pootsey', instead of the good old English 'foot', 'Aunty Paunty', 'Georgy Porgey'—a language which was 'a deleterious compound of low

Opposite: A 'physical force Chartist' arming for the fight that never was (1848)

'Members of the Begging Profession' (1849)

Dutch with ancient Syriac, and a spice or two of Arabic diluted in a river of polyglot'. Precocious children were equally repulsive.

Fond Mother: Why, he doesn't write very well yet, but he gets on nicely with his spelling. Come, Alexander, what does D.O.G. spell?

Infant Prodigy: Cat!

RATHER TOO MUCH OF A GOOD THING

We see advertised some 'Crying Dolls'. We must protest against this new kind of amusement. Just as if the real thing was not enough, but we are to have an addition to an evil, that is already sufficiently 'crying' in every household. We wish the inventor of this new toy (which might be called 'the Disturber of the Peace of Private Families') to be woke up regularly in the middle of the night, for the next twelve months to come, by one of his own 'Crying Dolls', and then he will be able to see how he likes it! Let one of the Dolls also be 'Teething'; for we should not be astonished now to hear of 'Teething Dolls', and 'Coughing and Choking Dolls', with other infantine varieties, and then the punishment of this 'monster in human form' will be complete. DR GUILLOTINE perished by the instrument he invented. The inventor of the 'Crying Dolls' deserves a similar fate.

1851

'How to make culprits comfortable; or, hints for prison discipline' (1849)

Next page: One of a series of cartoons in which Punch satirized the manners and customs of the middle classes (1849)

These infantile flights of perception were just too much for the genuine genius, doubtless a would-be contributor to Punch, who sits in an agony of deliberation at his table, distracted by his small son banging on a tin drum and his young daughter playing with the cat, while the discarded words overflow into the wastepaper basket. The wife of his 'bussum' has entered his study to say:

Oh, I don't want to interrupt you, dear! I only want some money for baby's socks—and to know whether you will have the mutton cold or hashed.

Every writer knows the feeling! His work might also be encouraged by juvenile parties which started at 8 or 9 pm and didn't end until one or two in the morning, a 'fashionable foolery of half killing children under the pretext of amusing them'.

Children did not improve as they grew up. 'The Rising Generation' portrayed in a series of cartoons, which started in 1847, the adolescent, second generation of the new middle classes, assured, demanding, impudent, many of whom were to perish later in the mismanaged gallantry of the Crimean War. A very small, young son stands in the man's place in front of the fire, warming his bottom, and addresses his outraged father, who has been quietly reading the newspaper:

I will tell you what it is, Governor, the sooner we come to some understanding the better. You can't expect a young feller to be

MANNERS · AND · CVSTOMS · OF · Yᵉ ENGLYSHE · IN · 1849 ·

AN "AT HOME",   Yᵉ POLKA.

No 2.

always at home; and if you don't like the way I go on, why I must have chambers, and so much a week.

Another juvenile wakes up his uncle for the fourth time. The uncle growls, 'Now then, what is it?'

Juvenile: Oh! just put a few coals on the fire and pass the wine, that's a good old chap.

A remarkably non-hirsute juvenile lolls in the barber's chair:

Aw, hairdresser, when you've finished with my hair, just take off my beard, will you?

The generation gap is of great antiquity extending back into the literature of classical times.

Punch also made fun of the 'growing evil' of moustaches and mutton chop whiskers among the older sons, and wondered whether cheap excursions to continental ports such as Boulogne was the cause of the growth in this 'Continental appendage'. The

---

THE SEVEN WONDERS OF A MARRIED WOMAN

1. Never having 'a gown to put on', when invited anywhere.
2. Always being down the first to breakfast! always being dressed in time for dinner! and never keeping the carriage (or the cab) waiting at the door a minute!
3. Not always having 'delicate health', about the autumn, and being recommended by her medical man 'change of air' immediately!
4. Keeping up her 'playing and singing' the same after marriage as before!
5. Giving her husband the best cup of tea!
6. Never making the house uncomfortable, by continually 'putting it to rights!'—nor filling it choke-full with a number of things it does not want, simply because they are 'BARGAINS'!
7. Never alluding, under the strongest provocation, to 'the complete sacrifice she has made of herself!'—nor regretting the 'two or three good offers', which she (in common with every married woman) had before she was foolish enough to accept *him*!!—and never, by any accident, calling her husband 'A BRUTE'!!!

1852

THE SEVEN WONDERS OF A MARRIED MAN

1. Not going to sleep after dinner!
2. Never going anywhere in the evening, excepting 'to the Club!!
3. Always being good tempered over the loss of a button, and never wreaking his vengeance on the coals if the dinner isn't ready exactly to a minute!
4. Never finding fault with his 'dear little wifey', if she happens to be his partner at whist.
5. Not 'wondering', regularly every week, 'how the money goes'.
6. Resigning himself cheerfully, when asked to accompany his wife on 'a little shopping'.
7. Insisting upon the servants sitting up, sooner than take the latch key with him!!!

1852

Continent was also blamed for the new fashion of dressing up pet dogs 'in the style of the *figurines* which profess to give the *Modes of Paris*'. But even that excess of femininity in canine fashions was preferable to the introduction from the United States of the new emancipated dress for women, designed by Mrs Amelia Bloomer. Earlier, Punch had sarcastically suggested that a female university ought to be established at the nation's expense, the University of Pimlico, with wenches instead of fellows—a Spinstership of Arts, and chairs of 'Sentiment, Flirtation, Poonah-painting and Cookery'. Now, Bloomerism produced a whole new crop of anti-feminist jokes and cartoons about emancipated women, both native and foreign, like 'the strong-minded American woman, Theodosia Bang M.A. of Boston' who wore bloomers, smoked cigars, asked men to dance, and sought the father's permission to marry.

It got just as much fun out of home repairs and improvements. Piped water supplies and fixed baths and shower units were only just being installed in middle-class homes at that time. Men, women and children all wore a new ablutionary uniform, consisting of a tall, dunce's, cone-shaped hat, which was worn in

Opposite: The man about town with moustache and mutton-chop whiskers—vintage 1849

Below: Home repairs could be just as expensive as they are now. A loose slate brought a whole army of workmen to make the necessary repairs (1849)

Advertisements.

IF Lord William Lennox will call at the PUNCH OFFICE, and ask for No. LXXXVII. of Punch, he will hear of something to his advantage.

WRITING.—Gentlemen, whose education has been neglected, are requested to try Gammon's *Grammatical Steel Pens*, which will write fluently upon any subject, with minute accuracy in the spelling and composition. Gammon's *Poetical Ink*, as used by the late William Shakspere, is strongly recommended to authors, as well as the *Patent Automaton Writing Machine*, which being wound up at night, and set to any particular style, will write articles upon any subject by the morning, at the rate of a sheet an hour. Strongly recommended to Magazine Contributors and the Anti-Corn-Law League.

À TOUS CEUX QUI DÉSIRENT APPRENDRE LE FRANÇAIS.—Plusieurs Messieurs, qui n'ont rien à faire, désirent employer leur temps à donner des leçons dans la Langue Française. Ou bien s'engager à traduire littéralement les ouvrages qui ont le plus de succès dès qu'ils sont publiés à Paris. S'adresser à la Société des Auteurs Dramatiques, à Trinity-court, Charing-cross, Londres.

RAPID COMMUNICATION WITH INDIA.—The aerial ship The Gull, will positively start in the course of the week from the London terminus, at the top of the Nelson Column. She is expected to make the voyage in three days, touching at Egypt for mummy-fuel. For fright and passage, apply to Captain Walker, Rasselas Terrace, Hoaxtown.

TRIUMPHS OF BRITISH VALOUR.

FAME'S trumpet says we've had victories enough,
And our great soldiers leave their arms to follow the plough.
The officers first, and then the Affghanistan chiefs,
All taken prisoners without asking leaf. [plete,
Then to London they come, with their retinues com-
Everybody makes a holiday to join in the *fête*.
Gents' clothes now are cheap, buy if you have not,
And go to Sholomansh's celebrated depôt.
For pages liveries and vests, with tunics and mournings
He'd like to loosh some monish wid you dis morningsh.
To suit all climates from Iceland to Ararat,
He'll dress you óut, for ready money, with éclat.

LIST OF PRICES.	£	s.	d.
Dress coats, warranted to wear three weeks	1	10	0
Do. trowsers, stylish plaid	0	9	6
Celebrated pervious Pilots, warranted to shrink from rain	0	12	0
Boys' fashionable Monkey-jacket Costume	0	7	0
Young Gents' Rob Roy dresses	0	15	0
Splendid Waistcoats, in the revolving bottle-jack style—new fashions	0	5	6
York Wrappers, in the last horse-cloth out-for-the-day half-price-to-the-play style	0	16	
Army Cloak, 9 yds. round, to hide seedy clothes	1	10	
Metropolitan Sporting Dress, for the fields in the suburbs of London (complete)	2	15	0
Fashionable Epping hunting-coat	1	10	0

Racket-blouses, and morning Tenterdens, adapted to gentlemen of the Queen's Bench.

A large assortment.   For ready money only.
Observe the Address, SHOLOMANSH, Cheap Tailor and Gout-fitter, City.

PUNCH'S DERBY SWEEP, 1843, is drawn this day, April 1. As no future subscribers will have a share in the winnings, but merely contribute their money, Punch will be glad of as many as he can get. Last horse to receive 10,000l., last but one 5,000l., and 1,000 pounds to be distributed amongst the horses who do not start.
This is the last that will be drawn, as sweeps are no longer allowed by Act of Parliament.

NERVOUSNESS.

PUNCH'S SPECIFIC for all kinds of Nervousness, Blue Devils, Hypochondria, &c. Sold in numbers at 3d., and volumes at 7s. 6d., at the sole depot, Wellington-street, Strand. None are genuine unless sold by our boy.

FAMILY MOURNING. — Ladies and Gentlemen obliged to go suddenly into mourning, will find the quickest method is to be dipped in the reservoir of the New Mourning Bath Establishment, Oxford Street. Re-transformation is effected in one minute, in a tank of Dr. Wynn's Reviver.

THE Shareholders in Waterloo Bridge are respectfully informed that a dividend of forty per cent. will commence to be paid on and after the 1st of April. The day having been fixed, due notice will be given when the year is finally agreed upon.

THE Creditors of the late Duke of York are requested to apply for payment of their claims to the keeper of the Column, who is charged with the care of the only available capital.

NEW PERIODICAL.

MEMOIRS OF THE MOULDY. Publishing in Weekly Numbers at threepence. By Joseph Mildew.
"Powerfully depressing."—*Literary Gazette*.

NEW WORKS JUST READY.

THE KITCHEN BLUE BOOK AND AREA COURT GUIDE. Compiled from the latest authorities. By the Editor of the *Morning Post*. Second Edition, corrected to April.
"This a useful work, containing the names of all the cooks, ladies' maids, and butlers in fashionable households; which only a long acquaintance with them could have accomplished. We recommend it to our readers."—*Evening Paper*.

NARRATIVE OF A RESIDENCE IN THE ROOKERY during the summer of 1842, with the Journal of an Attempt to Discover a Northern Passage from St. Giles's Church to the British Museum.
"This work displays a good deal of social observation, but the composition is defective; the execution is elaborate, but the characters faintly drawn. Upon the whole, however, it is an interesting book, although it has many faults."—*Spectator*.

TOOTHACHE EFFECTUALLY CURED. — Mr. Crackmolar, Surgeon Dentist, begs to introduce his newly-discovered Cure for this distressing malady. It allays all pain, prevents the progress of further decay, and entirely supersedes stopping or scaling, the patient experiencing instantaneous relief; at the same time the recurrence of the disease is effectually put a stop to. Unlike other advertised cures, some of which end in smoke, this will be found infallible, as it consists simply in extracting the offending tooth. At home from 10 to 16. Crackmolar's Artificial Teeth are warranted without springs or ligatures, and will keep for any time, provided they are never put into the mouth. N.B.—Mr. Crackmolar is a Member of the French Institute, to which learned body he proposed the cure of toothache by the guillotine.

In consequence of numerous complaints received from all parts of the country as to the difficulty in procuring the Weekly Numbers of PUNCH, the Proprietors have determined to print a STAMPED EDITION, (price 4d.) which may be sent free by Post, commencing with Number LXXX. It will be Published every Thursday Morning, and may be procured through any Newsman, or by direct application to the Office, No. 13, Wellington Street, Strand. In the latter case, a Post Office order for payment must be enclosed. As only a sufficient number of copies to supply the demand will be stamped, early application is particularly requested. The Publication of the Unstamped Edition, and of the Monthly Parts, will be continued precisely as heretofore.

Printed by Messrs. Bradbury and Evans, Lombard Street, in the Precinct of Whitefriars, in the city of London, and published by Joseph Smith, of No. 53, St. John's Wood Terrace, Regent's Park, in the Parish of Marylebone, in the County of Middlesex, at the Office, No. 13, Wellington Street, Strand, in the precinct of the Savoy, in the county of Middlesex.—Saturday, April 1, 1843.

the shower, and a long white cloak, which made them look, before their immersion, rather like dim members of the Ku Klux Klan. This passion for personal cleanliness and hygiene, which has been a characteristic feature of most ascending nations since the seventeenth century, was a great source of jokes about fat ladies who feared that they would become stuck in the narrow baths and about maids who interrupted paterfamilias while he was taking a shower.

Home repairs then produced no more pleasure than they sometimes do now in our 'do-it-yourself' age, as the long-lived and long-suffering cartoon character, Mr Briggs, discovered to his own nervous and financial cost after the cook had reported that a loose slate was causing dampness in the maid's room. Mr Briggs agreed to have it rectified. The builder assured him that it could soon be put right with a little 'compo'; but to Mr Briggs's astonishment, he awoke at five o'clock the following morning to find his house enveloped by wooden scaffolding and a whole army of Irish labourers, who were busily at work on the roof. When Mr Briggs climbed up on to the roof at midday to inspect progress in repairing the loose slate, he was informed by the persuasive foreman that, now they had started, it would be the easiest thing in the world to 'throw' his passage into the dining room and to build a new entrance hall with a slight conservatory over it, which would effect a marvellous improvement in his accommodation. Again Mr Briggs agreed. His house was thrown into such confusion by the work, with the old entrance blocked and the new one still unusable, that one day he was forced to climb in through the parlour window, and was caught in the act by a vigilant policeman. Even after all the improvements had been completed, his troubles did not cease, as the chimney had now started to smoke intolerably; but the builder assured him that it could soon be remedied and arrived one morning with another gang of men and a vast collection of cowls and other contrivances. Two months of domestic confusion—and the builder's bill—brought poor Mr Briggs to the verge of a nervous breakdown, so that he was forced to consult his doctor which meant a further bill. Even in those distant days, when workmen really *did* work, life could be no less intolerable, and expensive, for the long-suffering middle classes!

The state of London—its streets, its statues, its transport system, its public buildings—was also a matter of great concern. Punch was decidedly metropolitan in outlook then, even though as early as 1843 it had become so popular in the provinces that a stamped copy (4d post free) had been introduced to make it easier for country readers to keep in touch with all the excitements of the capital. At this period, Punch only made excursions to the country, to the seaside and to foreign parts, staying just long enough to see how Londoners behaved there or to poke fun at most of the people who had the misfortune to live there permanently. Its vision did not normally extend much further than fashionable suburbs, such

A page of mock advertisements (1843)

as Kensington, and its main interest was concentrated on a small segment of London bounded by Smithfield in the east, the British Museum in the north, Hyde Park Corner in the west and Westminster in the south. It knew every dislodged paving stone, every clock that did not strike, every crossing sweeper in its parish.

Nothing gives a better impression of what it was like to be living in London at that time than Punch. Historians may provide more facts; *The Times* may give a more comprehensive report; the *Illustrated London News* may furnish a more straightforward, graphic record; Dickens may capture the atmosphere of a limited segment of metropolitan life more vividly; but Punch alone, week after week, reproduces the feeling of the middle classes who lived in that age with all its current irritations, anxieties and absurdities. People do not live only at the peaks of history, though these are all registered in the pages; they live far more in the general trends of the immediate times, which can throb like some dull, depressing ache, or, in more open and expansive periods, can flow swiftly and clearly like an unimpeded stream. But people's transitory impressions of great events are always intermingled in daily life with an equivalent consciousness of the foibles, fads and fashions of the age. Life is experienced at many different levels simultaneously.

To open any volume, and to turn the pages, is to be transported back into those vanished times. Every November the fog closes in, a real pea-souper, with some pedestrians wearing the new fog glasses, guaranteed to make wearers see clearly in the deepest gloom. A blanket of silence settles on the dark streets at night, faintly lit by spluttering gas lights; the silence is broken from time to time by the rattle of some distant urchin's iron hoop, the clip-clop of horse's hooves, and a sudden eerie screech of a newly-invented fog screamer from a passing cab and the shout of a cabby, all masters of Cockney repartee, who were engaged in an unending battle with their middle-class customers. Further on, a London Peeler paces the pavement at his regulation two and a half miles an hour, dressed in his swallow-tail coat and tall top hat, which was not to be replaced by the more modern style of helmet until 1867. He rattles the iron gates of the area entrances, which have been firmly locked at 7 pm to stop any flighty maidservant escaping into mischief and to prevent any felon—or supper-seeking policeman—from entering. At night, the Bobby walks on the inside of the pavement; by day he walks on the kerb, so that, in an emergency, he can leap out into the road to restrain any bolting horse.

In the daytime, the streets of London would have exhibited to a present-day person a depressing familiarity and a great strangeness, with ladies in their long trailing dresses and their poke bonnets, which were to be replaced in a few years' time by broad-brimmed oversize hats; and young 'swells' in top hats and moustaches, carrying finely-furled slim umbrellas. A contemporary

Londoner, however, would have felt quite familiar with some aspects of the capital's life: the constant obstruction of the pavements; roads which were more fit for steeple chases than traffic; frequent traffic jams; and a bus service which was just as unsatisfactory as it is today. Victorian builders, no less than today's, had the annoying habit of claiming the liberty of the pavement for themselves, by boarding off whole sections, which they used as a gratuitous workyard or even, sometimes, as a 'pleasure-ground', as one outraged staff member must have discovered when he peered through a gap in the hoarding to discover a shop-keeper and some workmen engaged, not in urgent repairs, but only a quiet game of skittles.

The state of many of the capital's roads was deplorable. King's Road, Eaton Square, was a particularly 'chaotic highway' with 'carriages floundering through pools of slush and over mounds of earth, and horses plunging amid rubbish heaps sticking in the mud'. The filthy condition of the streets and the polluted water supplies caused repeated epidemics of cholera. To remedy this, many of the streets were being dug up in the late 1840s to install sewers and to repave the roads with wooden blocks. This work led to further obstructions and traffic delays; but Punch, with a typical English illogicality, an insistence on immediate convenience

---

SANITARY STREET NOMENCLATURE

The names of our London streets exhibit a disgraceful tautology. We are afraid to say how many Peter Streets, John Streets, and, above all, Wellington Streets there are in the metropolis. Let this fault be amended. Let the streets be called by their proper names; that is to say, at present, by the various nuisances or diseases which infest or pollute them, respectively. As, Open Sewer Street; Gully Hole Court; Slaughter House Buildings; Shambles Place; Knacker's Yard; Grave Yard Crescent; Charnel Square; Typhus Terrace; Scarlatina's Rents; Intermittent Row; Consumption Alley; Scrofula Lane; Cachexy Corner. Let such, at least, be the provisional nomenclature of the streets of London, till this filthy capital shall have been properly drained and watered; shall have had its churchyards closed, its atmosphere disinfected, and plague and pestilence expelled from its inhabitants.

A Movement in the Right Direction
Of all popular movements we do not know of one from which the public is likely to derive so much benefit and immediate improvement as the movement of all churchyards out of town.

Eau De Mort
We understand that the London Water Companies have been applied to by several farmers near the Metropolis for a supply of liquid manure, of which the water furnished by the Companies is said to contain all the ingredients.

1849

rather than future benefits, condemned both the cholera and the work which was meant to alleviate it. 'The usual blocking of London for the winter season has commenced at several points,' it commented one October, 'and the Strand is already in the hands of a hostile paviory,' so that vehicles were forced to make a detour of up to half a mile. Piccadilly had also 'fallen into the hands of the barbarians'. Traffic jams were also frequently caused by the huge advertising vans which lumbered slowly through the streets: they were particularly numerous at election times.

These 'repeated stoppages of the public thoroughfares' caused endless delays to the horse-drawn omnibuses, which were also frequently held up by acrimonious disputes over fares between passengers and the conductors, or cads as they were called then. Owing to the competition between rival companies, there were no fixed fares, which were controlled by 'the capricious taste of the conductor'. A fare, which had been quoted as twopence or threepence at the beginning of the journey, had often been doubled by the end, so that the passenger was faced with Hobson's choice of 'a fare of sixpence, and a fancied imposition, or else threepence, and a row thrown in'. The civility of the cads and of the drivers was related to the fare. 'How strange it is,' Punch commented, icily, 'that conductors never know how to conduct themselves.'

Punch also opposed the introduction of advertisements into

omnibuses, as there were already far too many, 'in all shapes, tricks and disguises' elsewhere. 'How will you like sitting for an hour opposite to a pleasant list of the wonderful cures by some Professor's ointment? Or, how will ladies like being stared in the face, all the way from Brentford to the Bank, with an elaborate detail of all the diseases which Old Methuselah's Pill professes to be a specific for?'

Many ingenious suggestions were made for the improvement of public transport: some visionary; others facetious, as Punch was no technologist. In 1846 it was proposed that 'those who are disposed to sink a little capital cannot do better than bury it under the Metropolis' by building a subterranean railway; the first underground railway between Paddington and Moorgate, using steam locomotives, was not opened until 1863, and the first deep-level electric Tube until 1890. It was also recommended that an overground, or aerial, omnibus line should be constructed, with mid-air stations on the top of the Monument, Nelson's column, and the arch at Hyde Park Corner; or, alternatively, that buses should be equipped with telescopic axles so that the wheels could run along the shop-window ledges which had previously been made of a uniform height. More facetiously, it was proposed that extendable ladders should be fixed on to the roofs of buses so that passengers stranded in traffic jams could escape through the second-floor windows of neighbouring houses, or that buses should consist of two or three storeys, containing reading rooms and hairdressing salons, where delayed passengers might while away the tedious hours.

There was an equal disenchantment with many other public aspects of metropolitan life: the slow delivery of the mails caused by Post Office 'apathy'; the excessive delays in compiling the catalogue in the reading room of the British Museum; the tardiness of Sir Charles Barry in completing the new Houses of Parliament to replace the old Palace of Westminster most of which had been destroyed by fire in 1834; the church clocks which never struck in unison; the fountains in Trafalgar Square, which never played; the careless cleaning of pictures in the National Gallery

'The real street obstructions.' Gigantic, horse-drawn advertising vans, sandwich-board men and young fruit sellers caused street obstructions in many parts of the capital (1850)

SPORTSMANLIKE OFFER

A very useful little book has been published, called, *How to see the British Museum in Four Visits*. Its success has induced the dauntless writer to undertake another guide—one for the accomplishment of a far more difficult feat. It is to be entitled, *How to find a Book in the Catalogue in Four Hours*. The promise is bold, and we suspend our judgment. The feat has never yet been performed; but this is the age of progress, even at the British Museum.

1852

ELECTRICAL CLOCKS

In Berlin they have Electrical Clocks—and in Stockholm, all the public clocks are put in motion by electricity. Why could not the same plan be adopted in London? By this means the various contradictions that exist amongst our public clocks might be remedied, and there would not be the difference of five hours, as there frequently is, between two clocks, in two neighbouring streets. We would not simply have our public clocks regulated in this manner, but also our private clocks. We do not see why the clocks on every floor, in every man's house, could not be brought under the control of electricity. Surely, it must be just as easy to lay on electricity as water or gas, and there is one comfort, that it would not cost one hundredth part as much.

1851

---

and the inability of the noble Board to distinguish a genuine Holbein from a fake; the Duke of Wellington's statue at Hyde Park Corner which represented 'a gigantic triumph of bad taste over public opinion'; the 'second-hand frippery' of Marble Arch, modelled on the Arch of Constantine, which was commissioned by George IV as a gateway to Buckingham Palace, and transferred to its present site in 1851; and the unhygienic state of Smithfield Market. It says something for English conservatism that some of these causes for complaint have not been rectified to this day. The Zoological Gardens was one of the few institutions to receive unstinted praise for its regular introduction of exotic animals, such as the hippopotamus and the orang-outang, 'the wild man of the woods'.

The music of the metropolis had diverse effects. The cornet-player practising at the open window, the untutored female pianist running up and down the scales next door, the itinerant Italians with their hurdy-gurdies, provoked as much irascibility as transistor radios and hi-fi equipment can do today. The Ethiopian serenaders, with their 'bones and banjos' who had 'darkened the metropolis' in 1847, were given a cautious welcome, until it was discovered that in some of them 'the darkness of the skin reaches no higher than the wrist, and goes no lower than the throat'. But the real musical heroine was Jenny Lind, the 'Swedish Nightingale', who made her London debut at Her Majesty's Theatre in 1847 in *Roberto il Diavolo*. No praise was too great, no hyperbole was too extreme for this twenty-seven-year-old soprano, this 'song bird of paradise'. Expectation had lagged far behind the exquisite reality. 'To call her the Swedish Nightingale is to put an extra feather in its cap—or tail—for the remainder of its existence.'

Jenny became the darling not only of the English stage but of the whole of fashionable society; but even the chorus of praise for her was far surpassed by the fanfare of triumph for the Great

Top: 'Cleaning the Pictures at the National Gallery' (1847)

Above: 'Punch presenting Jenny Lind with the Sovereignty of the Stage' (1847)

Exhibition, the apogee of this period, if not of the whole Victorian age. The idea had been conceived by Prince Albert; Samuel Plimsoll—of the Plimsoll line—was the honorary secretary of the organizing committee. Initial reaction had been none too favourable. Prince Albert found it difficult at first to raise money for his scheme, partly because of general doubts about its feasibility; partly because of his lingering unpopularity; and partly because England had not yet fully recovered from the financial crisis of 1847. This crisis, which was attributed to free trade, the failure of the potato crop and speculation in wheat and in railway shares, had caused bank failures, a cash shortage, price increases and retrenchment in public spending, a combination of events with which we are even more familiar today. There were also grave uncertainties about the exhibition hall itself, which was made of glass on a metal frame and was about a third of a mile long. Many people wondered if it could be built at all, and whether it would be of any use if it were erected. It was designed by Sir Joseph Paxton, a gardener turned architect, who had previously built the great conservatory for the Duke of Devonshire at Chatsworth. The difficulty of fitting it into any previously known architectural category caused Punch to suggest that it might be described as 'early English shed'. There were also fears that it would cost more to build than the estimated £10,000 (which would now buy a run-down semi), and that the site of Hyde Park would soon be overrun by 'tramp, vagrant and trull'.

None of these doubts and fears was justified. By 1850, prosperity could be seen around the corner again, which increased people's optimism and their willingness to subscribe and to buy season tickets. As the unusual building went up in Hyde Park and the official opening day of May 1, 1851, came nearer, anticipation and excitement mounted. Punch helped in no small way to ensure the success of the exhibition by its glittering choice of a popular name for the strange-looking building. After one or two false attempts, such as the 'Glass Palace' and the 'Great Glass Hive' it came up with the brilliantly appropriate 'Crystal Palace'. London's lodging-house keepers started to rub their hands with glee, when it was estimated that there could be as many as four million visitors. In fact, the estimates were greatly exceeded and there were over

---

THE RETURN OF PROSPERITY

Now matters are mending; our exports, ascending,
Cause Business to caper and Credit to crow;
Our fisheries are rising in manner surprising,
And butter is moving, and cheese on the go.
Up cordage has gotten, and fabrics of cotton
Exhibit an increase delightful to see;
Glass, hardware, and pottery, with drapery, silk-shottery,
And leather, are doing as well as may be.
Our dealings in linen give proof of a spinning,
Which all Europe's spiders can't equal us in;
We've sold the world metals for saucepans and kettles,
And had a proportionate influx of tin. . . .

1850

ONE TOUCH OF NATURE
MAKES THE WHOLE WORLD KIN!

'Dinner-time at the Crystal Palace' (1851)

six million visitors, many of them from the provinces and from foreign countries. The Great Exhibition of the Works of Industry of all Nations, to give it the full title, also attracted entries from many other nations. At least one million exhibits were sent in, but only a very small proportion of them could be included.

At the eleventh hour, there was one unexpected development, which could have marred the opening festivities, when the Executive Council decided that holders of season tickets (£3 for a man and only £2 for a woman in that unequal age), would not be admitted until just before closing time on the opening day. There were many protests. Punch believed that the decision had been calculated to please the Queen, but felt sure that it would disgust her. 'The idea of leaving her to ramble about the vast building in gloomy state, with a few gingerbread functionaries at her heels, is worthy of the imagination of the most sycophantic of snobs.' It could still be waspish when it wished.

The order was rescinded. At noon on May 1, to the cheers of the multitude without and to a flourish of trumpets from within, the royal couple entered the great crystal hall, where many dignitaries and some twenty-five thousand season-ticket holders were assembled. After the opening ceremony, the Queen and the Prince, holding the hands of their two oldest children, walked the whole length of the lower exhibition hall under the fond gaze of their admiring subjects.

The exhibition had an enormous impact on the whole nation in many diverse ways. One of the showpieces was the fabulous Kohinoor (Mountain of Light) diamond, which had been presented to the Queen by the East India Company in the previous year. But there were also many other exhibits to dazzle the sight in the thirty different categories into which they were arranged: new machines, strange inventions, attractive materials. Britain, which was then at the peak of its material prosperity and inventiveness, took many of the top awards. The exhibition demonstrated the immense superiority of the English nation in the many different branches of industry which it had been the first to develop, and symbolized its ostentatious wealth and new-found prosperity, particularly if you were a member of the middle classes and not a worker in the Potteries with the ever-present risk of lead poisoning; or a child of twelve or thirteen, working in a match factory, who had already contracted phosphorus poisoning, so that the vocal cords were being destroyed and the teeth were starting to fall out; or even a woman or a child working in an ordinary cotton factory who had to wait until 1874 before they gained a ten-hour working day after forty years or more of agitation. In reality, little had changed for the working classes; it was simply that their sufferings were less frequently recorded.

The exhibition did produce a slight change in attitudes. The organizers, in particular, and the middle classes in general, were amazed to discover that the respectable working men and their families who flocked into the capital from the north, were not so entirely different from other human beings as they had imagined. There was no vandalism or violence, only a few scraps of orange peel in the bowls of some fountains; the extra barriers which had been put up, and the extra policemen who had been called in, for the shilling entrance-fee days, were unnecessary. The Queen, who was delighted with her husband's success, and his general cleverness, visited the exhibition again and again, and in a truly democratic spirit actually made some of her visits on the 'shilling days'.

The exhibition increased the use of excursion trains and made them far more popular. It also boosted the reputation of the London Bobby, who had been unpopular with most social classes when the Metropolitan Police Force was formed in 1829. Through

'Whoever thought of meeting you here?' Social classes mingled more happily than was anticipated on the cheap entrance days at the Great Exhibition (1851)

their courteous control of the crowds and the cabbies, and their general affability, they started to gain a place in 'the affections of the people' and to create a new image for themselves. The exhibition brought about an even bigger change in the attitude towards Prince Albert. For two or three years previously, there had been some lessening of hostility, but the unexpected success of the exhibition, which made a profit of £250,000, gave him a far more secure place in the affections of the people. Punch commented wisely that he had 'earned imperishable fame for himself by an idea, the greatness of which, instead of becoming less, will appear still greater as it recedes from us'.

Many people wanted the Crystal Palace to remain in Hyde Park as a winter garden or as a permanent exhibition hall, which could have transformed the face of London by giving it a central pleasure place for the people in a green and open setting, but the forces of the establishment were too powerful. The nobility had only forsaken their exclusive rights to Rotten Row for five months as a concession to royalty and many of them wanted the building to be demolished entirely. As it was, it was removed piece by piece under the supervision of its architect to Sydenham, which was then a somewhat more fashionable place than it is now. On June 10, 1854, it was re-opened by the Queen as an exhibition and a concert hall, a function it continued to fulfil until 1936, when most of the Crystal Palace was destroyed by fire.

3 PEACE AND WAR

1852–1856

The Exhibition ushered in an era of unparalleled prosperity for England, the golden age of capitalism, which lasted for a quarter of a century. There was a rapid and almost unimpeded economic advance. Although there was some growth in the number of large companies, particularly after the passing of the Limited Liability Act in 1855, this was still very much the age of the small one-man business, the partnership, and the family firm. Their products had filled most of the stands at the Great Exhibition and they continued to prosper and to expand in this era of unrestricted competition, when their activities were still unfettered by the shackles of much legislation; when income tax was low; and when there were neither many large industrial combines on the one hand nor powerful trade unions on the other.

Although there were a number of small provincial unions, it was not until 1851 that the first of the new 'model' unions, the Amalgamated Society of Engineers, was formed for skilled craftsmen throughout the country. There was an initial trial of strength with the employers in 1852. Punch expressed no sympathy for the workers: 'the only strike workmen should ever be guilty of, is that recommended to all Englishmen in the song, "Britons, Strike Home".' In 1852 and 1853 there were a number of other strikes by dockyard workers in London, by policemen in Manchester, and by London cabmen, whose personal enterprise in overcharging their middle-class customers had resulted in the reformed parliament passing a law which restricted fares to sixpence a mile. On the whole, however, there was a long period of industrial peace until 1867.

The Amalgamated Society of Engineers established a pattern of quiet, respectable behaviour, avoiding strikes, settling disputes by talks with employers, and gaining whatever wage increases it could for its own skilled members. The same pattern of behaviour was adopted by the other national craft unions which were being formed in other industries such as building. This policy produced some improvement in wages for skilled workers but a much greater increase in affluence for many of their employers.

This was the great middle-class era. Punch, protesting all the time against the increased toadyism of the times, which made reference books relating to the peerage, baronetage and knightage best-sellers of this new 'snobage', stepped up another rung of the

FRUSTRATE THEIR NAVISH TRICKS

The only mode we can suggest for dealing with those persons who want so much public money as riggers of the Navy, is, to bring the rigour of the law to bear upon one or more of them. It would do no harm if a delinquent were to be transferred from a dock at Woolwich or Chatham, to the dock of the Old Bailey.

1852

STRIKING CIRCUMSTANCES

Really JOHN BULL may almost be described as a maniac with lucid intervals. He appears to be always suffering under some form of mania or other. A few years ago it was the Railway Mania—a very dangerous phrenzy. Then from time to time occurs a Poultry Mania, or one of the similar and milder forms of insanity. The mania now prevailing is one which, if not attended to, may perhaps prove troublesome. This is the Striking Mania. Everybody is Striking. The other day it was the cabmen; now it is the Dockyard labourers; the police, even, have struck and thrown down their staves. Our mechanics have so far become machines, that, like clocks, as clocks ought to be, they are all striking together.

Should this mania spread, we shall have Striking become what might be called the order, but that it will be the disorder, of the day. The professions will strike; you will send for your lawyer to make your will, and your messenger will return with *non est inventus—* struck; or should you ask the legal gentleman a six-and-eightpenny question, you will discover that he has struck for 13s. 4d. The physicians and surgeons will strike for two-guinea fees; the apothecaries for ten-shilling mixtures. The clergy will all strike—as indeed some of them, the poor curates, might reasonably do—and pluralists will be demanding forty thousand a year instead of twenty; whilst bishops will hang up the mitre, stick the crosier over the chimney piece, and hold out against the Ecclesiastical Commissioners for double incomes. In short, almost everybody will strike except the threshers, the smiths, and the pugilists.

With all this striking, though, we had better take care that we are not floored.

1853

ladder with the middle classes, some of whom had broken through the barrier, marked by an annual income of £2,500 or more, which enabled them to employ those ostentatious status symbols of the servant age; the footman in full livery. Jokes no longer related only to ignorant girls just up from the country. A cartoon of 1853, entitled 'Distressing Result of Emigration', showed two well-dressed ladies in a drawing room with attendant lap dogs and small children. One of them is saying to the other: 'Yes, my dear. John left us without any warning, and we can't match the other footman, because all the tall men are gone to Australia.' To escape

'Effects of a Strike, upon the capitalist and upon the working man' (1852)

Previous page: Balaclava harbour and camp during the Crimean War

from their life of servility, many of these handsome six-footers, who all had to match each other in height, had gone off to join the diggers after the discovery of gold in Bathurst, New South Wales, in 1851.

Punch changed with its readers. There was a hardening of arteries and of attitudes towards servants, workmen and beggars at that time. Downstairs maids, who, less than a decade before, had been the white slaves of England, had been transformed into the exploiters: real white slavery was now to be found in the drawing rooms upstairs. All beggars, even the 'deserving poor', like the unfortunate hand-loom weavers, had become suspect. These former 'aristocrats' of the working classes, who had at one time gaily and proudly walked the streets of northern towns with a five-pound note tucked into the bands of their hats, had been made redundant by the introduction of power-looms in factories. Their poverty and misery had been revealed in one government report after another; but even their genuine distress was cleverly mocked by the ingenious use of the theatrical aside in 'The Song of the Distressed Weaver':

Wearily spins the web of Life;
Dismally London's streets I tread:
I've got at home a consumptive wife,
And two small children lying dead.
(*Aside*) I must indulge a quiet grin—
I shall feel better when I've laughed;
My wife's at home consuming gin,
While the children sleep with an opium draught.

But to view this portion of the Victorian age, or indeed the whole of it, in terms only of a class struggle between the rich and the poor, is to falsify by simplification. There were other, darker forces at work, welling up spasmodically from the then largely unexplored regions of the subconscious, which were manifested in a variety of public and private forms: the intense preoccupation with religion, particularly the evangelical byways; the excruciating tortures inflicted by middle-class mothers on their defenceless children in the privacy of their homes; the barely concealed other world of eroticism and child-prostitution; the vicious bullying and flogging in public schools; the 'vapours' in women; the fascination among a minority with the occult, and new living forms; and the manias which regularly engulfed the capital, and sometimes, the whole country. Not all of these phenomena could be recorded in a respectable family magazine, but the cults and manias, which were particularly apparent in the years just before the outbreak of the Crimean War in 1854, were a suitable matter for treatment in what, with hindsight, now looks like a long journalistic 'silly season' extended from a few summer months to a few years. The season

---

PROSPECTIVE CHRONOLOGY

(From our own Clairvoyant)

1855. City Improvement Act passed.
1857. Temple Bar pulled down and Lord Mayor's Show abolished.
1880. Peace established with the Caffres—for a month or two.
1890. Library Catalogue of the British Museum completed—to the letter D.
1899. Sale of *Uncle Tom's Cabin* ceases.
1900. COLONEL SIBTHORP becomes Premier, by virtue of his seniority.
1901. Attempted revival of Protection fails.
1953. New National Gallery opened.
1960. Beer Monopoly ends.
1975. Westminster Bridge rebuilt, and the New Houses of Parliament finished.
1999. Railway accidents cease.
2000. Income-tax removed.
Date not Fixed. Prosperity of Ireland begins.
Date too remote to be calculated. Publication of *Punch* ceases.

1853

There was little sympathy for the men who tried to escape poverty at home by joining in the gold rush overseas (1852)

REAL WHITE SLAVERY

We have heard a great deal about White Slavery, but the real White Slaves of the present day are the fair housekeepers of England, who, though nominally mistresses, are in fact the slaves of those who, under the name of domestics, exercise a domestic tyranny over them. The 'Servants' Bazaars', as they are called, are daily lined with well-dressed victims, termed by bitter courtesy 'mistresses', who are waiting to be 'engaged' by a variety of females, who, under the assumed denomination of 'servants', are pleased to make choice of the families they will condescend to go into.

The following are a few snatches of conversation picked up in a Domestic Bazaar on a recent occasion.

Lady. You will of course have your own bed to make.

Plain—disgustingly plain—Cook. Make my own bed, Mum! I never heard of such a thing. You won't suit me, Mum.

Second Lady. You would have to answer the door while the man is dressing.

Second Cook. Oh, dear me, Mum! I couldn't think of walking up and down stairs; your place, I see, is not the kind of thing for me, Mum. . . .

1853

even had its own Loch Ness Monster, the wider-ranging American sea-serpent, reported to be over a hundred feet long, which was sighted in places as far apart as the Irish coast, Delaware Bay and the Pacific Ocean!

Many of the cults also originated in the United States, which was to many English men and women then a land of boastful exaggeration. Modern spiritualism had started there in 1848 and one of the most celebrated American mediums, Stainton Moses, had visited England to help establish the London Spiritualist Alliance. But the claims of mediums to contact the other world through trances and table-rapping seemed as extravagant to Punch as Mrs Bloomer's under-garments. The public, however, was interested and visits by American mediums, such as the mythical 'Mrs Dorcas A Juggles', attracted large audiences. Experiments with electro-biology (the Victorian spoon-bending) in which tables moved and hats whirled without any apparent human intervention, became fashionable in London drawing rooms for a time.

There was an increase in the number of astrologers, 'knaves who pretend to read the stars for fools'. A poultry mania caused sheds to be hastily erected in many grounds and gardens, as chicken-keeping became 'as fashionable as crochet' and 'every well-regulated young lady keeps her Cochin-China in preference to a canary'. Fine specimens of the Cochin-China breed changed hands at enormous prices for those days of up to £75 apiece. Vegetarianism started to gain new adherents and there was also a great increase in the number of teetotalers, a movement which had also started in the United States in 1827, when some members of a temperance society signed a 'T' or 'total' pledge to abstain from all alcohol. Under the influence of native nonconformists and evangelicals, and the stimulus of visiting lecturers from the United States, the temperance movement grew rapidly in England, so that the first branch of a Band of Hope for children had already been started in Leeds by 1847, and the strongest drink that could be obtained in the refreshment room of the Great Exhibition was ginger beer. There was also a vigorous anti-smoking campaign with well-meaning young ladies forming societies to ban smoking, described by one such lady as 'a nasty, odious, dirty, filthy, disgusting and most objectionable habit.' But vegetarianism, and temperance in smoking and in drinking, had little fundamental appeal then to the beef-eating, bibulous John Bull. By nature and tradition, he was also opposed to the growing sabbatarian movement, though it gained a number of considerable victories at that time by enforcing the Sunday closing of many shops and public places of instruction and entertainment, including the National Gallery and the British Museum, and by making Sunday a day of dismal idleness in many middle-class homes.

These manias were supplanted by more primitive passions with the approach of war. The Eastern Question—'Drat the Eastern

Railway official: 'You'd better not smoke, Sir!'
Traveller: 'That's what my Friends say.'
Railway official: 'But you *musn't* smoke, Sir!'
Traveller: 'So my Doctor tells me.'
Railway official (indignantly): 'But you *shan't* smoke, Sir!'
Traveller: 'Ah, just what my Wife says!' (1852)

Question', wrote Punch in 1853—dominated English foreign policy in the nineteenth century. Turkey, whose empire at the beginning of the century had extended right round the eastern littoral of the Mediterranean and the Adriatic, from Jugoslavia in the north to Egypt in the south, had become the sick man of Europe, unable to retain its grasp on its imperial domains. England feared that Russia would seize this opportunity to extend its influence in the area and advance towards Constantinople and the straits of the Bosphorus and of the Dardanelles to give its Black Sea Fleet an outlet to the Mediterranean where English interests and sea routes might be threatened.

War broke out between Turkey and Russia in September, 1853. The Turkish fleet was destroyed off Sinope in the Black Sea in November. Although England was still deeply suspicious of its traditional enemy, France, and of its despotic ruler, Napoleon III, who had taken the title of Emperor in 1852, the two countries were united in their hostility to Russia and both of them sent warships into the Black Sea as a warning.

As it became increasingly apparent that England might have to go to war with Russia, a jingoistic fever infected the nation. Big manoeuvres involving the Guards, the Cavalry and the Artillery, were held at Chobham Camp, in Surrey, in July 1853, and the next month the Queen reviewed the Fleet at Spithead. A minority was

VICTORIA!

Fight—with determined fury fight!
We know that we are in the right,
For Freedom's holy sake we rise,
And have the best of battle-cries—
      VICTORIA

Fight for the QUEEN in the QUEEN'S own name,
'T is an omen of conquest, an earnest of fame,
On with it, brave men, through smoke and flame!
      VICTORIA! VICTORIA!

We arm against a despot's reign,
The empire of the scourge and chain;
Of Liberty we wage the war,
Old England's QUEEN against the Czar;
      VICTORIA!

Fight, mindful of our old renown,
To put a brutal monster down,
Fight in the name of BRITANNIA's Crown,
      VICTORIA! VICTORIA!

In numbers let the villain trust;
His savage hordes shall bite the dust,
Splitting the liar and scoundrel's ear,
Scatter his host with our English cheer—
      VICTORIA!

They in the righteous cause who die
Triumphant fall, and, where they lie,
Let their last faint breath swell the cry—
      VICTORIA! VICTORIA!

1854

opposed to war. Richard Cobden and John Bright, who had been the darlings of the middle classes during their earlier fight for the repeal of the Corn Laws, were now reviled for their policy of peace at any price and were branded as traitors when they formed a Peace Society. Punch struck a medal in its pages for a 'Peace Assurance Society' showing the Chobham manoeuvres on the face and the Spithead review on the reverse. Armed strength, and not conciliation, was the best deterrent.

In times of peace, the wealthy caste of army officers with their affected speech, their ostentatious living, and their passions for egg-throwing and moustaches, were not particularly popular among the English public, which had a long-standing aversion to standing armies. A pre-war cartoon showed two cavalry officers in front of their mess fire, one a lieutenant and the other the cornet who carried the colours:

Lieutenant Blazer (of the Plungers): Good Gwacious! Here's a

READY AYE READY

SPITHEAD . AVGVST 1853

The magazine's own medal for the 'Peace Assurance Society' (1853)

horwible go! The Infantwy's going to gwow a moustache!

Cornet Fluffey: Yaw don't mean that! Well! There's only one alternative for us. WE must shave!!

But with the approach of war, all, or almost all, was forgiven and the concealed reverse of the medal was displayed: the coolness under fire, the stiff upper lip, the general *sang froid*, and all that. An officer, who has been posted to the Near East, is saying to a girl in a drawing room: 'Of course, it's rather a bore just at the beginning of the season—and I shall miss the Derby! Wish they could have had the Russians over here because then we could have thrashed 'em in Hyde Park, and dined at Greenwich afterwards, you know!'

National conflicts were then still seen in ancient, metonymical terms. It was obvious that the Russian bear needed 'his nails cut' before he did some injury either to himself or to anyone who happened to go near him; therefore the British lion had to be awakened and unleashed:

> They've roused thee then at last,
> Thou old, majestic beast;
> Did they think thy strength was past
> Because thy roar had ceased?

England and France declared war on Russia in March 1854. The

THE HOUSE OF INTERESTS

Of what is the House of Commons made?
Of Members for Land and Members for Trade,
Of Members for Cotton and Timber, and Ships,
And Members for Stocks and Shares, and Scrips.

The House has Members for Foundries and Mines,
And Members for sundry Railway Lines,
And Members for Sugar, and Tea, and Spice,
And Members for Pepper, and Paddy, and Rice.

The House of Commons is not without
Members for Ale, and Beer, and Stout;
And Members for Whisky and Members for Gin
The House of Commons there are within. . . .

It has plenty of mouths to talk and prate:
But where are the heads to rule a state?
They'll preach and prose till all is blue,
But which of them knows the thing to do?

The Hour has come, but not the Man,
Find him inform us where we can!
Where we cannot 'tis very plain;
In the House of Commons we seek in vain.

1855

Crimean War was the only major European conflict in which
Britain was involved from 1815 to 1914. British and French troops
who had originally been stationed in Bulgaria, landed on the
Crimean peninsula in the Black Sea in September and achieved an
initial victory over the Russians in the battle of the Alma, which
opened the way to the main Russian stronghold and naval base of

Opposite: 'How the Holy men of
Russia inspire their soldiers'
(1854)

Above: 'Our Guards. They can
play; and, by jove, they can fight
too' (1854)

IMPROVEMENTS FOR THE ARMY

WANTED.—A few decrepit, spiritless old men, to command HER
MAJESTY'S troops. Any superannuated General Officer, whose
faculties are impaired, and who is as infirm in body as he is feeble in
mind, has now an opportunity of glory and distinction together with
pay. A title and the order of G.C.B., will be the sure reward of
incompetency and failure. Apply to SERJEANT HARDINGE, the
Chequers, near the Horse Guards.

It Speaks for Itself

It is said of LORD PANMURE, the new War Minister, that in
consequence of his being liable to periodical attacks of the gout,
there are many times when he cannot be spoken to for three weeks.
Perhaps this may be looked on as one of his chief qualifications for
his post at the present moment; for if a War Minister cannot be
spoken to for three weeks all chance of having awkward questions
put to him will be avoided.

1855

Sevastopol. But that early promise of victory was not to be fulfilled. As the troops settled down to the long siege of Sevastopol, the astonishing mismanagement and stupidity of the high command, and the incompetence of the prime minister, Lord Aberdeen, were gradually revealed to an increasingly horrified nation. That great war correspondent, William Howard Russell of *The Times*, supplied the facts about the disasters in the Crimea; Punch added the invective.

The fourth Earl of Aberdeen, educated at Harrow and Cambridge, was a weak, idle, impulsive man, possessing none of the political skills of his mentor, Sir Robert Peel. Palmerston, the Churchill of the Crimean War, who succeeded Aberdeen as Prime Minister in February 1855, at the age of seventy, had dismissed his predecessor as 'antiquated imbecility'. Punch satirised Aberdeen mercilessly in many cartoons: one showed the steps of No 10 Downing Street littered with the words 'delay', 'twaddle', 'disorder', 'blunders' and 'incapacity'.

The high command of the army was no more competent or effective. Field Marshal Viscount Hardinge, Commander-in-Chief of the Army, was nearly seventy years of age when war broke out, and sat securely 'in his own temple' in the Horse Guards, like Mars. 'Lady—we beg pardon—Lord Hardinge' was little better than a 'myth' and was 'not fit to be any Chief at all, except we may say, Chief Pensioner of Chelsea Hospital.' The one-armed Lord Raglan, who commanded the army in the field, was afflicted by a grave loss of memory about all recent events, though 'he remembers a great deal that occurred during the Peninsular War'. In his despatches from the front, he displayed all the typical English passion for discussing the weather when there was nothing else to talk about. The antiquated admirals of the fleet were no better equipped to serve in the stormy seas of the Euxine. The appointment in 1855 of a new admiral, who was only fifty-four years of age, caused ironic protests:

> We have come to a pretty pass indeed, when mere boys, who have never known what the gout is, and can venture on deck probably without the aid of a crutch, are given the command of a fleet, and this, too, when we have admirals on the list of the matured ages of seventy, eighty, and ninety—steady-going, experienced men, who can neither see, hear, talk nor walk!

On the British side, the Crimean War was one long chronicle of almost uninterrupted disastrous mismanagement and inefficiency. Many transports sank in the violent tempests in the Black Sea and even when supplies did arrive they were often useless, provoking disparaging comments among the troops, and doubtless, far coarser protests, which, of course, had to go unreported in Punch. One consignment of woollen drawers, sent out to keep the soldiers warm in temperatures of twenty below, had been manufactured for boys of seven to ten years of age! The kilts of Highland troops were

Opposite: 'You are requested not to speak to the man at the wheel.' The Prime Minister, the Earl of Aberdeen, in his tartan stockings, was reviled for his lethargy and lack of spirit in the early years of the war (1854)

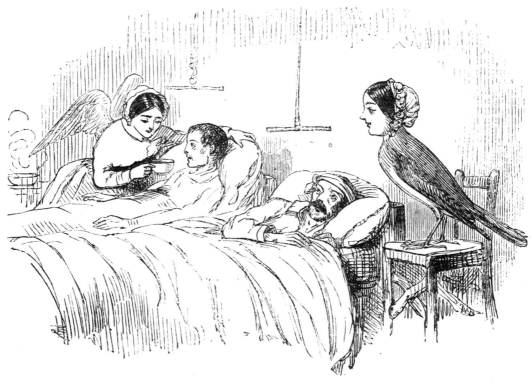

not replaced by warm tartan trousers until 1855. Native inventiveness eventually produced some remedies: the cardigan, named after the Earl of Cardigan who led the Charge of the Light Brigade, and woollen Balaclava helmets both date from this time.

Although some cowardly officers—no gentlemen—had sold their commissions to avoid being posted to the front, there were many individual acts of great heroism, which were recognized by the institution of the Victoria Cross in 1856, the highest British decoration for signal valour or devotion to the country in the presence of the enemy. The most famous act of unnecessary gallantry occurred during the battle of Balaclava in October 1854, when, owing to a misunderstanding of orders, the Light Brigade, the 17th Hussars, charged up a long valley against the full force of the Russian artillery. A third of the Brigade were killed or

Opposite above: The Charge of the Light Brigade. The original caption read: 'A Trump Card(igan)' (1854)

Opposite below: Florence Nightingale (1854)

Right: 'General Février turns traitor.' During the bitterly cold winter of 1855, the Tsar, Nicholas I, had boasted that 'Russia has two generals in whom she can confide—General Janvier and Février'. He died in February (1855)

wounded. One of the French allies, with Gallic logic, commented, 'It was magnificent, but it is not war.' Incompetence in the high command called forth thousands of acts of great individual bravery in the ranks below. When Captain Ellison, of the Fusiliers, found that his ammunition was exhausted, he ordered his men to use stones against Russian guns!

Those soldiers who were wounded by Russian bullets, or were infected by cholera and dysentry through British filth, had little chance of recovery in the insanitary, understaffed, overcrowded base hospitals at Scutari. The status of doctors in the British army was low. While doctors in the French army were treated with respect and given the highest honours, British commanders, with far less regard for their soldier's lives, treated 'a regimental surgeon as doing a lowish kind of duty, even when performing a capital operation with a cool head and a steady hand amid a shower of bullets'. It was no different at Scutari, where there was a great shortage of food, pure drinking water, clothing, and medical supplies. As a consequence, the mortality rate there in the early months of the war was 42 per cent. In October 1854, Florence Nightingale, the daughter of wealthy parents who had named her after the Italian city where she had been born, went out to Scutari with a party of forty volunteer nurses. Her untiring work in caring for the sick and the wounded, in improving essential supplies and in cleaning up the insanitary wards, was largely responsible for reducing the mortality rate to 2 per cent.

Although her devoted and unselfish work captured the imagination of the nation as it has done ever since, even she could not escape calumny in that age of religious bigotry. The evangelicals of Exeter Hall suspected her of preaching 'Romanism' to dying soldiers, because she had a close friend who was a Puseyite; while more middle-of-the-road Christians accused her of being a Unitarian! The Queen recognized her great service to the state by sending her a jewelled ornament just before the conclusion of the war. Punch suggested, without success, that it might become the germ of a new order, the 'Order of the Nightingale'. Meanwhile a grateful nation had subscribed £44,000 to a special fund, which Florence Nightingale used to open the first English training school for nurses, at St Thomas's Hospital, London, after she had returned from the Crimea, travelling incognito, as 'Miss Smith' to avoid unwelcome publicity.

Sevastopol fell in September, 1855 and peace came in the following February. Bungling continued to the end, marring the victory celebrations, as the train taking MPs and other dignitaries to Southampton for the review of the fleet was late in arriving, and the tenders to take the VIPs out to the warships were also late and insufficient in number. Punch suggested that the illuminations to celebrate the peace might show at Chelsea Hospital, 'a dissolving view of a brigade of cavalry, gradually melting to a skeleton of a horse'; at Horse Guards, Britannia with her hands bound by red

Punch rings in the peace with the Russian bear (1856)

tape; and at the Admiralty, an illuminated view of Balaclava Harbour, which might be transformed with little alteration into a view of Southampton Docks.

England had been humiliated, not so much by the Russians, as by the example of its French allies and even more by the incompetencies of its own leaders. This had been acknowledged by Palmerston, who had ordered an official day of humiliation and

The craze for fast bowling prompted Punch to design some protective clothing (1854)

fast in April, 1855, shortly after assuming office. Punch did not welcome this initiative. It published a cartoon showing Raglan fast asleep and commented: that was 'humiliating—very'.

CURIOSITIES OF LONDON

A good cigar bought at a Betting Shop.
A playbill that spoke the truth.
A fresh-laid egg that was less than a month old.
A statue that was an ornament to the metropolis.
A glass of London porter that had not been doctored.
A shilling that had been refused by a box-keeper for a seat at the theatre.
A quiet street without an organ.
An omnibus that was not going to start directly.
A bargain, bought at an 'Awful Failure' shop, that did not turn out a do.
A policeman with spectacles; a blue-coat boy on horseback; a chimney-sweep with an umbrella; a quaker with a bull-dog; a fountain that was not supremely ridiculous; a Leicester Square foreigner that looked happy; a Belgravian Jeames in a hurry; a bishop carrying a baby; or a beadle in a balloon.
And lastly, a paving stone of solid gold, the same as the streets of London are proverbially paved with.

1855

Although English pride had been wounded, the general tenor of lives on the home front had not been too greatly disturbed, except for relatives of the fallen. There were, however, some unpleasant side effects. It had been suggested at one point that a bachelor tax should be introduced to help pay for the war: instead, income tax was increased to the unprecedented height of 6.6 per cent, though it was halved to its normal level again in 1857. As always happens in wartime and emergencies, some profiteers made vast fortunes out of the misfortunes of others. The price of sugar rose steeply in 1855, after two or three speculators had cornered the market, and bread prices also rose. Violence had increased at home, as it frequently does in wartime. The streets of the capital became even less safe at night with a great increase in the crime of garotting, in which the victim was throttled with a rope before he was robbed. To give some protection a device was invented, consisting of a wide collar with long protruding metal spikes. In a less harmful way, the cricket fields of England were afflicted by a violent passion for fast

Large hats became fashionable during the Crimean War. The original caption read: 'Dearest Rosalind, how delighted I am to meet you! One moment later, and my new bonnet would have been utterly ruined' (1855)

bowling; while rivalry between mothers was increased by the introduction of the 'baby show abomination, which had its origin in the vulgar brain of a greedy American quack'.

There were great changes, too, in fashion. During the war, women's hats had expanded to enormous sizes; but it was not until the end of the war that women adopted the crinoline and started to dress 'not in the height, but the full breadth of the fashion'. Their exaggerated shapes were achieved by wearing special petticoats with sewn-in metal hoops, or by wearing a wire cage, which was attached to the waist by tapes. This strange fashion, which combined both a *noli me tangere* look and a grotesque emphasis of women's wider pelvic regions, symbolized precisely the ambiguous Victorian attitude to sex and birth: frilly pantaloons were also worn to prevent any chance display of shameful leg. The mania for -

---

HOW TO WRITE THE BIOGRAPHY OF A WOMAN

An impudent fellow says: 'Show me all the dresses a woman has worn in the course of her life, and I will write her Biography from them.'

1853

The new fashion of the crinoline sometimes made social intercourse rather difficult (1856)

'The patent anti-garotte overcoat.' One enterprising gentleman uses his wife's crinoline as a protective device against the current street crime of garotting (1856)

the crinoline lasted for a decade. Punch, which knew a good joke when it saw one (sometimes too well), went on laughing for an equivalent number of years at women who could not get into a railway carriage, cabs, or theatre seats, and were so greatly inconvenienced by the exaggerated fashion that two of them could not enter a room together, or sit on the average-sized sofa, at the same time.

THE WOMEN AND THE ELECTRIC TELEGRAPH

The Electric Telegraph Company has organised a band of female Clerks to work the Electric Telegraph. It is a happy idea to turn the gentler sex to account by employing the ladies in a task which will give full scope to their love of rapid talking. We have known and (unhappily) heard tongues that can go at a tremendous rate, but to talk as quick as lightning is a luxury that the women have not yet been able to enjoy, and we doubt not that there will be a rush of gratuitous Clerks, when it is generally known that females may have the opportunity of talking by Electric Telegraph.

1854

4 ALICE IN CRINOLINELAND

1857–1867

The Crimean War was only a brief interruption, a distant storm, in the long midsummer of the Victorian middle classes, when the days were all long and languorous, and the nights could be extended interminably by dinner parties, and dances, and even grander balls; when the whole of life, for a time, at least, seemed to be safe and secure, particularly for nice, respectable girls like Ann and Alice, or Mary and Sarah, in their gilded wire cages. Oh, it was so pleasant and exciting just to be alive! These young ladies lived in large town houses or rambling country mansions which could be rented or leased in those days for a few pounds a week, their minds scarcely ruffled by any problem more vital than the choice of a gown for next week's ball, or whether the new curate would be more handsome than the last.

Their labours were as insignificant as their thoughts, for Alice, and her kind, definitely did not wish to work. Sometimes when Alice's papa was feeling grumpy, which, fortunately, was not very often, he would start complaining about the income tax, which had reached 4 per cent by 1860, and her expensive tastes in clothes, and say that he would have to send her out to work; but Alice thought he was only joking, at least, she hoped he was.

WHAT MAY BE DONE IN FIFTY YEARS

An American paper is eloquent upon the many inventions and discoveries for which the world is indebted to the first half of the nineteenth century. Amongst others, may be enumerated the following:—*Punch*, steamers, railways, the electric telegraph, gas, photography, and chloroform.

The second half of the nineteenth century scarcely promises to be so rich. Its claims to originality do not, at present, extend much beyond—Crinoline, all-round collars, peg-top trousers, perambulators, penny ices, halfpenny steamboats, and penny papers. The list is not a lively one.

However, there is plenty of time between this and the commencement of the twentieth century. The next forty years may witness the birth of some tremendous genius, who may hit upon the means of setting the Thames on fire; or, for aught we know, abolishing the National Debt. All things are, we believe, possible to the genius of Man, even down to the completion of Trafalgar Square!

1859

She thought it must be really horrid to work. This had happened to a friend of hers, who had been forced to take a situation as a governess after her father's bank had failed. Alice thought it must be very trying to look after other people's children; your own younger brothers and sisters were quite bad enough. And governess's salaries were very low, not much more than the wages of her own maid. Alice remembered reading one advertisement, republished in Punch, seeking a governess to instruct eight children (mainly boys) at a salary of £20 a year, and another offering £30 a year for teaching four children 'good English, correct French and music'. She thought that Punch, which she read occasionally, was quite justified in calling these advertisers 'insolent snobs', for they must certainly be people of uncommonly low birth to offer such small salaries for those great accomplishments which would have been far beyond her own capacities. Although Alice couldn't understand all of Punch, particularly when it used such long words, she liked the pictures very much, especially the nice, kind ones about young ladies which, curiously, always seemed to refer to her.

It was true that there were a few advanced young women who actually wanted to work, like Elizabeth Blackwell, the very first female doctor in the world, who had qualified in the United States in 1849, and had become the first woman doctor to register in her native England ten years later. But Alice thought she could never learn enough to become a doctor herself and in this view she was still supported by many men, including the Edinburgh College of Physicians who had rejected the idea of training women doctors by a majority of eighteen to sixteen in 1862. The Earl of Shaftesbury, who was always meddling, had helped to start a Society for the Employment of Women two years before that. But Alice agreed

Previous page: A middle-class wedding party of 1865

Left: 'The safest way of taking a lady down to dinner.' Punch continued to make fun of the crinoline throughout the years that the fashion lasted (1864)

JUVENILE JOKES

Intelligent Pet: 'Ma, dear, what do they play the organ so loud for, when church is over? Is it to wake us up?' (1867)

Cousin Lizzie: Now, Charles, when you are near me, you really must not go on your knees! People are sure to make remarks. (1867)

Fascinating Gent. (to precocious little girl): You are a very nice girl; you shall be my wifey when you grow up—
Little Girl: No, thank you; I don't want to have a husband; but Aunt Bessie does; I heard her say so! (*Sensation on the part of* AUNT BESSIE) (1859)

Lover: What a bore! Just as I was going to pop the question to Jenny Jones, here's my nurse come for me. (1858)

Innocence: And did you ask any little girls to your wedding, mamma?
Mamma: Yes, dear, several little girls.
Innocence: And, pray, why didn't you ask *me*? (1866)

with Punch that it would be very silly to have young ladies working as printers, book-keepers, post-office clerks, hotel manageresses and law clerks, when there were a sufficient number of men to perform these tasks quite adequately. No, it was definitely better for the whole nation if a young lady did not soil her delicate hands with work, even in her own home, for if Alice had cleaned her room and tidied it, instead of leaving it in a state of great disorder with all her discarded clothing scattered carelessly over the furniture and the floor, there would have been no work for the housemaids and her own maid, and what would they have done, then, poor things, as there was almost certainly no other employment for them.

Young ladies were not born to work but to marry—the higher the better—as her own mamma was always observing. That was why it was particularly important for them to present their best possible appearance at all times. Oh, she had seen such a funny joke once about a girl who had fallen asleep on a sofa and had been surprised by her fiancé, while she was, yes, actually, snoring. How mortifying that must have been! Alice prayed that nothing quite so catastrophic would ever happen to her.

Young ladies had to been seen in the right places; at the right time; and in the right fashion which was then the crinoline. Alice knew that it was dangerous to wear this contrivance. She had read

Opposite: This was the era of the juvenile joke:
First juvenile: 'I wonder what can make Helen Holdfast polk with young Albert Grig?'
Second juvenile: 'Don't you know? Why, to make me jealous! But she had better not go too far!' (1858)

THE BEST SEWING-MACHINE

The very best Sewing-Machine a man can have is a Wife. It is one that requires but a kind word to set it in motion, rarely gets out of repair, makes but little noise, is seldom the cause of dust, and, once in motion, will go on uninterruptedly for hours, without the slightest trimming, or the smallest personal supervision being necessary. It will make shirts, darn stockings, sew on buttons, mark pocket handkerchiefs, cut out pinafores, and manufacture children's frocks out of any old thing you may give it; and this it will do behind your back just as well as before your face. In fact, you may leave the house for days, and it will go on working just the same. If it does get out of order a little, from being overworked, it mends itself by being left alone for a short time, after which it returns to its sewing with greater vigour than ever.

Of course, sewing machines vary a great deal. Some are much quicker than others. It depends in a vast measure upon the particular pattern you select. If you are fortunate in picking out the choicest pattern of a Wife—one, for instance, that sings whilst working, and seems to be never so happy as when the husband's linen is in hand—the Sewing Machine may be pronounced perfect of its kind; so much so, that there is no make-shift in the world that can possibly replace it, either for love or money. In short, no gentleman's establishment is complete without one of these Sewing Machines in the house!

1859

Opposite above: The first 'lady-physicians' appeared at this time; but Punch suspected that some men chose to use their services for the pleasure of their company rather than for reasons of health (1865)

Opposite below: 'A case of real distress. Flora can see a letter from *him*, but cannot get it for at least ten minutes, because Pa has the key.' Poor Flora! (1865)

Above: 'Utility combined with elegance' (1858)

in Punch how three thousand women in England and Wales were burnt to death every year; and twenty times as many injured, through wearing it, or highly flammable muslin. It was easy to set your skirt on fire when you were walking past an open grate and almost impossible to extinguish the blaze which fed on the great balloon of air entrapped by the distended skirt. There were also perils at the seaside, when the crinoline, acting on the same principle as a kite, sometimes lifted its wearer bodily from the promenade on windy days and deposited her screaming in the rough seas below.

Punch was highly critical of this 'suttee system' which condemned so many women to an early, and unnecessary, death. After Alice had asked her clever, older brother the meaning of 'suttee', she decided, quite crossly, that Mr Punch, who was usually kind, sweet Mr Punch, was for once quite wrong. It should have been quite obvious to him that no fashionable young lady could afford *not* to wear crinoline, even if it did result in your premature decease. Alice was quite prepared, if necessary, to make the final sacrifice, for the greater glory of the womanhood of England, just like those brave women who had been hacked to death by cruel natives at Cawnpore during the Indian mutiny. Mr Punch might just as well ask her to give up dancing, archery, croquet or hunting.

The name of the game was not croquet but love for Clara. The original caption read: *Chorus of offended maidens:* 'Well! If Clara and Captain de Holster are going on in that ridiculous manner—we may as well leave off playing' (1863)

It was always a pleasure for Alice to ride—side saddle, of course—to hounds, for she knew that she looked at her very best in her tall, black hat set at a slight angle above her dark tresses, and her tight-waisted riding jacket suited her to a degree, she felt sure; furthermore, it was a privilege to take part in this 'manly, healthy pastime', in which the skill and stamina of the riders was tested. That was the only kind of equality she desired. Toxophily, with all its romantic associations and opportunities, was becoming popular everywhere, particularly in the neighbourhood of barracks. What young heart did not flutter and beat faster on seeing a flight of arrows, with all their romantic symbolism, and which maiden's cheek did not blush with pleasure at the dream of gaining their match prize, a bracelet or a necklace, presented by the officers of the regiment? Croquet was another great delight. Everyone who was anyone, and Alice was certainly that, now played croquet on their lawns, which were given over almost entirely to this skilful and entertaining pastime during the fine summer months. Alice knew that she would never forget those long, idyllic afternoons, undisturbed by anything but the clicking of the long-handled wooden mallets against the croquet balls, the approving cries for some especially skilled shot, and the openly admiring glances of that particularly handsome captain. She always felt that she presented her very best appearance on the

'Well, ladies and gentlemen.
I s'pose this is what *you* calls
pleasure and comes all the way
from London for?' (1865)

croquet ground; sporting and healthy, yet somehow delicate and
refined at the same time. She did not, however, favour the new
sport of rolling skate, preferring the more conventional, and
graceful, skating on ice. Yachting was even less appealing to her.
It was quite impossible to look your best when you were huddled
up against the wind on a cold, and often wet and slippery deck: in
addition there was also the frightening possibility of being sick.
Poor Alice could hear the guffaws of laughter that *mal de mer*
always provoked, and almost went green at the very thought.

PROFITABLE PARTNERSHIP

We have heard of two brothers (their united ages do not exceed 27,
and their united heights cannot soar much above 5 feet 10) who have
gone into partnership at the West End. They have commenced
operations at the corner of two fashionable streets. One is a
Crossing-sweeper, and the other is a Shoe-black. Their places of
business, are, you may say, next door to each other. The first dirties,
as though by accident, the boots of those Swells, who do not give him
anything, as they step over his crossing, and the second comes in for
the benefit of cleaning them. In this way, they play into each other's
hands, and divide a considerable sum at the end of the day.

1857

In fact, if she was honest, which she always tried to be, she didn't care very much for the seaside at all. Of course, you had to go to a resort once a year because it was the fashion; but secretly she found the seaside rather boring. There was very little of interest to do; she missed her friends; and you could not even while away the boring hours by reading, as the circulating libraries always seemed to have so few books, and they were mainly quite unreadable. Furthermore, the wind always chapped her skin and the sun reddened her nose, spoiling her delicate complexion of which she was so proud. She liked the sea bathing, but once you had left the privacy of the bathing machine, and descended the little wooden steps into the water, you were very likely to meet the impudent stares of some horrid, low-born men (real snobs) who had rowed out specially just to catch a glimpse of you in dishabille. Alice thought that men of that kind were quite disgusting; they really ought to be given a good ducking.

It was strange, she thought, how the number of snobs, blackguards and agitators seemed to be increasing as the years passed. They could appear in many different guises: crossing sweepers, those 'whining mendicants' who plundered the nervous, and molested the brave by splashing their dresses with mud if they did not receive a coin; squatters who took over other people's houses while they were away on holiday and were almost

'Snobs at the Seaside', the perils of sea bathing (1865)

'Common objects at the sea-side—generally found upon the rocks at low water' (1858)

WARMTH FOR WILFUL NAKEDNESS

Now that the inclement season of the year is approaching, our sympathies are naturally excited on behalf of those poor creatures whose clothing is insufficient to protect them from the wintry blast. Just at this time no conduct can be more unseasonable than that of able-bodied paupers in workhouses, who, on purpose to give trouble and annoyance, tear up their clothes. Still, they should not be left to perish of cold; and magistrates ought to be empowered by statute to order the backs of all such perverse offenders to be warmed with a good whipping.

December 23, 1865

NO MORE PROPERTY

Hooray! No more law, no more order, no more nothing! Society may now be considered as at an end, and everybody may take care of himself. The dissolution of all conventional arrangements is complete. Hooray! Government—there is none now—had long been preparing us for this, and SIR GEORGE GREY's determined refusal to interfere with highwaymen and garotters was but a part of the system. The right of the strong hand is now fairly proclaimed and recognised. The final proofs have just been given. Some people thought they should like a house in Stamford Street. It belonged to somebody else, but what of that? They broke the door open, and nobly took it. Some other people thought they should like a house in Eaton Square. It belonged to somebody else, but what of that? Besides, she was out of town, and what business had she to keep a house half empty? They turned her servant into the street, and took the house. Hooray! In each case, the ridiculous rightful owner, as she called herself, appealed to the Magistrate, and a mere form of reprobation was gone through, but SIR GEORGE GREY will, of course, take care that no punishment is inflicted. . . .

1863

encouraged to do so by the inactivity of the Home Secretary, Sir George Grey; and, worst of all, garotters, those murderous brutes, who had become so numerous and self-assured that they now perpetrated their dastardly crimes in broad daylight. It had become impossible 'to walk in safety from one street to the next' or to go into Hyde Park without having your pocket picked, or to enter St James's Park on a Sunday without 'being hustled by the roughs from St Giles's'.

Flogging for robbery with violence had been introduced in 1863, but it had done little to stop these dreadful attacks, even though nineteen men had been scarified in the first year, including 'one young villain' of nineteen, who had been given fifty lashes and four years' penal servitude in Liverpool. Punch had suggested that photographs should be published as a warning to others showing the 'contorted' faces of these young brutes as they were being flogged; but her own dear papa went even further, and thought that they should be given a taste of their own medicine by borrowing a garotte from Spain and strangling a few of them, which might be even more salutary in its effects than introducing them to the tenderer mercies of Calcraft, the English hangman.

Sometimes the whole world seemed to have become topsy-turvy, more and more like that illogical world portrayed in *Alice's Adventures in Wonderland*, a book which Alice had bought for her small sister when it was first published in 1865, but which she was even fonder of reading herself. Alice, who had the good habit of asking herself questions, often wondered why confusion and violence seemed to be increasing as she became older; but she had never found an answer which gave her complete satisfaction. For a long time, she thought it must be because there were so many people in the world who had had the misfortune not to have been born in England. That theory certainly solved the German problem to her complete satisfaction, as the Prussians had always been noted for their warlike qualities, which was why Bismarck had gone to war with Denmark in 1864 over Schleswig-Holstein (though she was rapidly forgetting whether that was the name of a person or a place) and with Austria two years later. Oh, how funny Mr Punch had been about Bismarck's wish to build a navy, when everyone who was anyone knew that there was only one real navy in the whole wide world; but, Bismarck was entitled to have his little rowing boats, his 'fleet of the future' if he wished, and the English would even build it for him, as it was certain that the Germans could not build it as well for themselves.

The Irish were a different case and far worse. There were very few peoples in the world who had been presented with the unique privilege of giving up their own nationality and becoming English; but, instead of being eternally grateful, the Irish, who were a most unstable people, had done nothing but create trouble ever since. First, it had been O'Connell; then it was Young Ireland; and now it was the Fenians, who were, of course, supported in money, words

'Going out to tea in the Suburbs'
(1863)

and deeds by the Americans, who were turning out to be almost as bad as the Irish.

The Americans had already gained their precious freedom, so why did they need to make idle threats against England every few years? It served them right that they were now fighting among themselves. Alice didn't know very much about the American Civil War. The Yankees had always seemed bad enough to her, but the Confederates were even worse, confederates as Mr Punch had said, in nothing but 'the crime of upholding slavery', which had been abolished in England years before. Publicly, Alice subscribed to the idea that all men were her brothers, though she had never met a black man, and had no particular wish to do so; but, secretly, she doubted if it could really be true. She had certainly giggled for days after she had read a poem in Punch 'written' by the gorilla in the London Zoo, who was depicted with a placard round his hairy neck asking if he was also a man and a brother. She thought it must be extremely bewildering to be born black, instead of white, like her and all of her friends, and it could have been scarcely less strange to have been born yellow. Alice felt sure that the colour of the Chinese helped to explain their jaundiced views. Their jealousy was always causing trouble, as it had done in 1857, when they had murdered all the white passengers and crew on the mail boat between Hongkong and Canton, simply because the English

ANOTHER GROSS OUTRAGE ON AMERICA

An American Gentleman has been denied admission to the Opera, because he was not dressed in the Opera costume. He was attired in nankeen trousers, a striped waistcoat like a livery servant's, a blue-fogle handkerchief, and had on a pea-green cutaway coat with brass buttons as big as cheese-plates. In vain was it represented to him by Mr. NUGENT, and other gentlemen, connected with the theatre, that the above articles of dress were against the sumptuary laws invariably enforced at that aristocratic establishment; the American gentleman only stormed, and raved, and blustered; and, after many loud representations that he was 'a free and enlightened citizen of the United States' (everyone present admitting the extreme freedom, but no one allowing him the smallest ray of enlightenment), he declared that if he came in a smock frock, or even in a bathing costume, they had no right to refuse him admission. These propositions were strongly disputed, and, on the free and enlightened citizen's becoming a nuisance, he was civilly shown the door that leads to the nearest police-station. The American Minister was present in the Theatre at the time, and, upon being told of the above incident, left in great dudgeon.

1856

Opposite: 'The "sensation" struggle in America.' Punch's view of the American civil war (1862)

Below: Darwin's revolutionary theories that the apes were mankind's predecessors and 'brothers' found little favour (1861)

had been kind enough to take over Canton from the Chinese to give them the increased benefit of English trade.

Alice's theory about foreigners seemed to be quite tenable, until similar unreasonable creatures started to appear in England. In 1866 some workmen in Sheffield blew up the houses of fellow workers who had refused to join their union: a very curious way of demonstrating brotherly love and unity, Alice thought. At first, she comforted herself with the thought that they might be Irish, for she knew that the Irish were always using explosives, and that many of them had come over to England to work because they had created so much confusion and poverty at home. But later on in the same year, there had been riots and bloodshed in Hyde Park, the scene of such peaceful harmony between all social classes only fifteen years before, as workmen demanded the right to vote. These workmen were indubitably as English as their leaders, that 'constitution-wrecker', John Bright, and 'the illustrious Edmond Beales (M.A.)', who had been educated at Eton and Cambridge and was obviously, as her own papa frequently declared, a traitor to his class. Workmen were given the vote in the following year. Disraeli had steered the Bill through the House of Commons which was just what you might expect from a 'time-server of thirty years' standing'. They would certainly have never been given the vote if Lord Palmerston—good, old Pam—had still been alive; but he had died in 1865, wise, patriotic and statesmanlike to the last.

If workmen wanted to demonstrate, Alice thought, there were much more worthy causes. She was, therefore, delighted to read in Punch that there were still some sensible workmen in Worcester,

THE 'SPECIALS'' PROCLAMATION;

OR, TWO WRONGS MAKE ONE RIGHT.

We have hitherto believed this logical contradiction to be beyond the possibility of any other solution; but we live in strange times, which produce results of a like character. The proclamation below speaks for itself; it is composed of two Fenian proclamations; (Manchester and Clerkenwell) and when read separately there can be but little doubt about there being two outrageous 'Wrongs;' but let them be read as one whole Specials' Proclamation, (as 'Hurrah for old England') and it cannot be denied that they are one 'Noble Right.'

Hurrah for	Old England
Fenianism	Is a curse
We fight for	The QUEEN and Constitution
The Fenian brotherhood	Is a league with Satan
We love	Free Speech
This Rebellion	Is treason
We glory in	a Free Press
Shooting and plunder	Will not be tolerated
We will not fight for	The 'Centre's' freedom
England's welfare	must be secured
We must succeed	at every hazard
The Union	We love
We Love not	Such wreck and waste
And never said	Let the Union sink
We want	The Union
Foreign intervention	cannot be allowed
We cherish	The British Flag
The Emerald green	Is a flaunting lie
We venerate	The powers that be
Fenian Chivalry	Is hateful mockery
Down with	Mob Law
Law and Order	Shall Triumph.

Vivat Regina!

1868

In their campaign to get the vote, workmen demonstrated in Hyde Park. The original caption read: 'Ruffianly Policeman about to perpetrate a brutal and dastardly assault on the people' (1866)

three or four hundred in all, though she thought there must be many more like them in other parts of the country, who had demonstrated in 1865, not in favour of the vote, which they could use only every seven years, but for cheaper meat, which they wanted to eat every day. Punch was quite right to declare that this was the kind of agitation which would be supported by the whole nation. Drought and cattle disease (and profiteering butchers, of course, who were the 'real rinderpest'), had sent the price of home-produced beef soaring to the scandalous height of fourteen pence a pound, so that many people could no longer afford to buy it. Even her own mamma had decided to try the new jerked beef from La Plata, which had been dried and dehydrated in the hot South American sun; but cook was so disgusted with this 'shoe-leather', as she called it, that she threatened to find a new situation if she was ever subjected to such trials in her own kitchen again.

VINTAGE JOKES

Irascible Old Gent: Waiter! This plate is quite cold.
Waiter: Yessir, but the chop is 'ot, Sir, which I think you'll find it'll warm up the plate nicely, sir! (1866)

Dainty Old Gent: Have I liked my Dinner? No, I have not. So don't give what I've left to the Cat, Sir; because as she's sure to become pie, I should like her to die a natural death, and not be poisoned! (1861)

Sir William: Swiggles! What induced you to put such wine as this before me?
Swiggles: Well, you see, Sir William, as *some*body must drink it,—and there ain't none of us in the Hall can touch it!! (1860)

CHRISTMAS AT THE CRYSTAL PALACE

We were told the other day of a Frenchman who had brought his wife and family to England that they might spend their Christmas at the Crystal Palace. The notion at first struck us as being rather curious, but on afterthought we deemed it a most sensible idea. We doubt if France, with all her forests, could show a Christmas-tree full sixty feet in height; and we feel quite sure that France, with all its skill in cookery, could not boast of such roast beef and mince-pies and plum-puddings as it is the privilege of England to produce. We remember to have heard of an unlucky fellow-countryman who, being doomed to pass a Christmas-day in Paris, devoted all his energies to make sure of a plum-pudding; and who, having himself purchased all the requisite ingredients, felt tolerably easy in his mind for the result. Well, Christmas Day arrived, and after a first course of cow beef cut in strips, up came the plum-pudding, served in a tureen; for the cook, not being told to boil it in a cloth, had omitted so to do, and thereby turned it into soup. . . .

1861

That, Alice decided, was what was wrong with servants and workmen; they always thought they were the only people who had problems. They never appreciated the far greater difficulties of their superiors' lives. There was poor papa, for example, who had really become rather stout, despite all his hard work and his worry about his great business responsibilities; but had, nevertheless, bravely decided that, fairly soon, he must adopt the diet recommended by the London undertaker, William Banting. Alice wondered how cook, who was always stealing the best cuts off the joint and stuffing herself with potatoes, would like to go on such a starvation regimen.

Servants had such an easy, secure and luxurious existence, living rent-free in other people's homes, that they never understood the problems of real life. Cook was so satisfied and self-fulfilled that she had never even bothered to marry. Poor Alice wasn't in that happy situation. She was getting on in years—she

Top: *Guard:* 'Smoking not allowed, gents.'
Swell: 'O! Ah! What's the fine?'
Guard: 'A shilling, ready money, to the guard, Sir. Forty shillings to the company, payable by instalments at your own convenience' (1865)

Above: *Advanced young lady:* 'Will you take a cigarette, Captain de Robynsone?' *Captain:* 'Thanks, no! I have not learned to smoke yet. But pray go on; smoke does not make me at all ill—I rather like it' (1865)

knew that—and she had to find a husband fairly soon, as her mother was always indicating. You could, of course, marry for money, but Alice had too much liking for romance to do that. On the other hand, she certainly didn't want to marry on £300 a year as some people had already done, which really did show how dreadfully hard life was becoming for the middle classes. Punch had published so many funny jokes and cartoons about that subject, including one showing a juvenile warming his hands in front of the fire and saying, 'Why, it ain't enough to buy a fellah

101

CORPORATION REFORM

'Oh! that this too, too solid flesh would melt!' is the bootless exclamation of many who, like *Hamlet*, are 'fat and scant of breath.' Among them, for several years, appears to have been numbered the author of a little pamphlet now before us, entitled *Letter on Corpulence, addressed to the Public* by WILLIAM BANTING. . . . His sight beginning to fail, and his hearing to be impaired, after having, as aforesaid, consulted numerous practitioners to no purpose, he at last 'found the right man', who put him on a plan of diet which we proceed to transcribe in his own words for the benefit of *Punch's* numerous readers, who laugh and grow fat:—

'For breakfast, I take four or five ounces of beef, mutton, kidneys, broiled fish, bacon, or cold meat of any kind except pork; a large cup of tea (without milk or sugar), a little biscuit, or one ounce of dry toast.

For dinner, Five or six ounces of any fish except salmon, any meat except pork, any vegetable except potato, one ounce of dry toast, fruit out of a pudding, any kind of poultry or game, and two or three glasses of good claret, sherry, or Madeira—Champagne, Port, and Beer forbidden.

For tea, Two or three ounces of fruit, a rusk or two, and a cup of tea without milk or sugar.

For supper, Three or four ounces of meat or fish, similar to dinner, with a glass or two of claret.

For nightcap, if required, A tumbler of grog—(gin, whisky, or brandy, without sugar)—or a glass or two of claret or sherry.'

MR. BANTING, by the observance of this diet-scale, than which, as he justly observes, 'that man must be an extraordinary person who would desire a better table', has been 'reduced many inches in bulk, and thirty-five pounds in weight in thirty-eight weeks'; has got rid of all the special inconveniences of obesity, has had his sight restored, his hearing improved, and his 'other bodily ailments' greatly 'ameliorated'.

1863

cigars.' Not that she would ever want to marry a man who smoked. Alice really disliked those selfish men who, in spite of prospects of a forty-shilling penalty, lit up their cigars and pipes in railway carriages. She was even more opposed to those advanced young ladies who had taken to smoking cigarettes, sometimes in public, but more often in secret, while mamma was absent so that they were forced to chew a scented pastille afterwards to conceal the odour on their breath.

No, Alice wanted nothing more than a simple, conventional life, with three or four servants, a house with four or five bedrooms, and a handsome, loving husband with a sufficiently large salary, supplemented perhaps by an allowance from a relative, to keep her in the style to which she was accustomed. It wasn't very much to ask. Given that, she would not object too strongly if her husband wanted to go off from time to time to do his duty with the

A FEW SIMPLE REASONS AGAINST SMOKING

By the Mother of a Large Family, and the widow of
three husbands, who all Smoked.

1. Because it injures the curtains.
2. Because it is injurious to the furniture generally.
3. Because it is not agreeable to breakfast in the room when the gentlemen have been smoking overnight. . . .
4. Because no man's temper is better for it the next morning.
5. Because it keeps persons up to late hours, when every respectable person ought to be in bed.
6. Because the smell haunts a man's clothes, and his beard, and his hair, and his whiskers, and his whole body, for days afterwards—so much so that it is positively uncomfortable sometimes to go near him.
7. Because it is a selfish gratification that not only injures those who partake of it, but has the further effect of driving the ladies out of the room.
8. Because it is, also, an expensive habit which the ladies, not participating in its so-called enjoyments, cannot possibly have the smallest sympathy with or appreciation for.
9. Because it has the further effect of making gentlemen drink a great deal more than they otherwise would, and so weakens their purses besides ruining their constitutions, to say nothing of the many comforts and new dresses that their dear wives and children may have been unjustly deprived of, supposing the same amount of money had only been judiciously laid out at home.
10. Because it gives extra trouble to the servants who have to clean and to ventilate the rooms the next morning.
11. Because how are one's daughters to get married, if the gentlemen are always locked up in a separate room paying court to their filthy pipes and cigars?
12. Because it unfits a young man, who is wedded to it, for the refining influence of female society.
13. Because it puts a stop to music, singing, flirting and all rational enjoyments.
14. Because it is a custom originally imported from the savages.
15. Because we see the nations that smoke the most are mostly the stupidest, heaviest, laziest, dreariest, dreamiest, most senseless, and worthless beings that encumber—like so many weeds only capable of emitting so much smoke—the face of the earth.
16. Because when a man says he is going out to smoke a cigar, there's no knowing what mischief he is bent upon, or the harm the monster may be likely to get into.
17. Because it is not allowed in the Palace, or Windsor Castle, or in any respectable establishment.
18. Because the majority of husbands only do it because they know it is offensive to their wives.

And a thousand other good reasons, if one only had the patience to enumerate them all. Pray did ADAM *smoke?*

1861

Opposite above: Chignons were the latest fashion in hairstyles at this time (1866)

Opposite below: Victorian ladies were deeply shocked by the 'indelicate' knee-length clothes of fisherwomen when they went abroad for the first time (1866)

Above: Women were often more interested than their bored husbands in viewing the scenery on foreign tours (1864)

Volunteers, for she thought that men always looked much more handsome in uniform.

'The only thing I shall insist on', she said to herself, 'is that we spend our honeymoon abroad.' A honeymoon at an English seaside resort would have bored her greatly; but she had always wanted to visit France, even though her clever, older brother warned her that all Frenchmen were nothing but 'hairy mossoos'. It would be nice to be married, she decided, as she fingered her dark tresses. Perhaps she would have her hair dyed yellow, which was now becoming quite fashionable, or wear a chignon. She wondered which would suit her best, as she fell asleep gracefully, without snoring.

5 RETRENCHMENT AND REFORM

1868–1874

The languorous, lambent days of middle-class midsummer had ended with squalls over Sheffield, turbulence in Hyde Park, distant thunder in Austria, and an approaching depression over the Atlantic. There was a growing awareness that the lazy, drifting days were over, that hatches must be battened down, and quickly, too, if the storms ahead were to be negotiated successfully.

LITERARY SMASHERS

Another villainous case of word-coining is reported from America. A person there is spoken of as having 'suicided'. The coiner of this verb no doubt belongs to the vile gang who lately issued the word 'burgle', meaning to commit a burglary, and the still more hideous terms 'excurted' and 'injuncted', which have recently been suffered to pass current in the States. In the same false mint, we doubt not, have been coined such words as 'cabled', 'wired', 'donated', 'deputated', 'interviewed', 'orated', 'reliable', 'rendition', 'walkist', 'eatist' and the like, with which the Queen's English has lately been in Yankeeland defaced. Such wretched counterfeits as these for genuine sterling English are, with scarcely an exception, first uttered in the newspapers; and if editors declined to pay for any article wherein they detected this false coinage, the literary smashers would be literally smashed.

1870

OUR BRUTAL CUSTOMS

An 'ANGLO-INDIAN' in *The Times*, complains of the vexatious detention which he, and a lot of other passengers who arrived, the other Saturday night by the *Malta* at Southampton, endured owing to the brutality of the Customs' authorities of that port. From what 'ANGLO-INDIAN' says, it certainly does not appear that those officials are accustomed to execute their odious office more offensively and injuriously than the rest of their tribe, who, however, everywhere, are well known to make a point of inflicting on travellers, whom it is possible for them to impede and plague, no less of delay, trouble, and annoyance than they possibly can. A competitive examination in civility is desirable for candidates for place in the Customs' department of the so-called Civil Service. If existing Custom-house officials had to undergo that ordeal it is to be feared that they would be nearly all of them plucked.

1872

Previous page: Heavy traffic on
London Bridge in about 1870

Below: Arrival of the boat from
Boulogne at Folkestone (1873)

The achievements of some other European countries had started
to make English eyes blink with envy and to provoke an
unaccustomed feeling of inferiority, which was by no means
mollified on the return to Folkestone by the inevitable confrontation with the 'brutal Customs', who were waiting, if they
deigned to do so, on the quayside. The French, who had been
disparaged as 'hairy mossoos', were now venerated for their
magnificent achievement in rebuilding Paris, which had been

carried out by Baron Haussman at the enormous cost then of £34 million, equivalent to half the total British annual revenue. Imagine what Baron Haussman might do with London, Punch said jealously, if he were made Lord Mayor with plenary powers to rebuild and to improve. 'What a widening of narrow streets, and sweeping out of holes and corners, and pulling down of ugly old buildings, and sending to the right-about of vested rights and interests would infallibly ensue.'

But the roads in London remained a disgrace, causing businessmen to lose both their time and their temper daily. Although the English people continually boasted of being practical, they were 'either too stingy or too stupid' to provide themselves with 'good thoroughfares and roads'. The smooth Parisian roads were constructed with the aid of steam-rollers. 'What fools the French must think us, when they see us strewing lumps of granite loosely in our roadways, and wearing out our carriage wheels in grinding it to slush.' Yet it was not until 1868, when the rebuilding of Paris had been almost completed, that the London Commissioners of Sewers decided to use asphalt for the building of the capital's roads. 'Fancy London without mud! What a blessing to look forward to.'

At home the English middle classes ate French food, particularly when they were giving their dinner parties, even though some of them did not really like French food and many of their self-instructed cooks had scarcely any idea of how to prepare it. Even so, the middle classes as a whole, did at least pay their gastronomic respects to what was undoubtedly a much superior *cuisine*. On their foreign travels, however, they were already becoming embarrassed by the chauvinistic contempt for foreign foods displayed by some of their compatriots, unabashed provincial 'vulgarians' with a belief in the vast superiority of the English sausage, even though that item, like much English food of the time, was often grossly adulterated. Punch published a joke in 1869 showing a bearded tourist in an Alpine restaurant saying to a clean-shaven 'Kellner' who is offering him a plate of sliced sausage:

I say, old feller, any 'osses died about 'ere lately?

Cheval morts, you know!!

(The title was apposite: *Why we are so Beloved on the Continent.*) Punch was also impressed by the contrast in the culinary skills displayed by ordinary housewives on different sides of the Channel:

> How to make the pot boil is with many a poor labourer, a vastly puzzling problem; and his wife is quite as puzzled to find out what to put in it. A French peasant can make soup, and a score of toothsome dishes, while an English one can only serve up half-boiled cabbage and potatoes.

Prussian might was another source of even greater disquiet and concern. The Prussians had been the first nation to adopt the

The English middle classes were notorious abroad for their reserve and shyness. The original caption read: 'Sketch of a bench on the boulevards, occupied by four English people who only know each other by sight' (1870)

breech-loading rifle; its great superiority over the old-fashioned muzzle-loader, which the British army still used, had been demonstrated with deadly effect in the quick victories over Denmark in 1864 and over Austria two years later. But the increasing naval strength of Prussia was even more alarming to England, whose first line of defence had always been the sea. Punch, as it openly admitted, had liked to poke fun at the Prussian navy—'the solitary gunboat on the Spree'—but, meanwhile, the Prussian 'Fleet of the Future' had been transformed into 'The Fleet of the Present', composed of a very respectable force of steam-driven iron-clads. England had its own iron-clads, the first of them, the *Warrior*, having been launched in 1861; but they were unsteady even in moderate seas. In 1868, Punch warned: 'Our big men-of-war in armour, which cost half-a-million each, are said to be as useless and unhandy in a sea-way as the obsolete old men-in-armour who adorn the Lord Mayor's show.' And two years later, as if to prove Punch right, the *Captain* overturned and sank with the loss of all its crew in a moderate gale.

There was another serious defect. The English warships still had fixed guns like those in wooden ships, which could only fire broadside, while the guns in other nations' warships were mounted in rotatable turrets, like those which had first been used by both sides in the American Civil War. Foreign warships could fire in all directions at a rate of six shots to every English one. If England did not build turret ships soon, Punch declared in 1868, France, the United States, or even Germany would rule the waves in place of Britannia. 'The wooden heads that constitute our Admiralty Board' were 'even more obsolescent than the country's old wooden walls.'

As a result of this unpreparedness, and even more through its traditional policy of trying to evade involvement in continental conflicts, England was happy to stand on the sidelines during the Franco-German War of 1870 and to adopt a posture of 'perfect impartiality' in this struggle between the 'Prussian Pot' and the 'French Kettle'. It was somewhat less happy to settle the Alabama dispute with the reunited U.S.A. in 1871 by paying £3,250,000 compensation for the havoc that the *Alabama*, built by Britain for the Confederate states, had wreaked among Union merchant ships

Although Punch adopted an impartial attitude towards the Franco-Prussian War in its written comment, the cartoons did not always reveal the same views. Here the Germans are depicted as the aggressor (1870)

during the American Civil War; but this was all part of Gladstone's policy of 'peace, retrenchment and reform'.

William Ewart Gladstone had become prime minister for the first time in 1868 at the age of fifty-eight. The country was in desperate need of a purge, the process of purification which is essential for every generation. Gladstone's administration, the greatest reforming ministry of the whole Victorian age, dosed the nation with a number of measures which helped to cleanse it of much injustice, inefficiency and backwardness. Gladstone himself had proclaimed that his mission was 'to pacify Ireland'. The Anglican church in Ireland, a long-standing source of grievance in a predominantly Catholic country, was disestablished in 1869. In the following year, Gladstone tried to solve the land problem by the Irish Land Act, which made landlords compensate evicted tenants who had made improvements to their farms; but landlords easily evaded the provisions of the Act by raising their tenants' rent to such an impossibly high level that they were forced to leave.

In 1870, the Education Act started the State system of education;

Gladstone 'taking the (Irish) bull by the horns' (1870)

THE UNCIVIL CIVIL SERVICE

It is a subject of very general remark, that it is difficult to find a subordinate in the Civil Service who has got a civil tongue in his head. The Post Office authorities have hit upon a happy expedient at the Money Order Office in Charing Cross, where written directions are placed in front of the bars, behind which the bears are to be heard growling out their indistinct replies to any question which may be addressed to them. We recommend everyone who applies for a money-order at Charing Cross to read the written directions, if he wishes to avoid the surliness and snappishness to which he will probably be exposed, if he ventures to ask one of the Civil servants a civil question.

1855

---

competitive examinations replaced political patronage for entry to the Civil Service, making what you knew more important than who you knew; and the Married Women's Property Act gave the 3,200,000 working women the right to keep their own earnings which, previously had belonged by law to their husbands. In the following year, trade unions were granted full legal recognition: the Universities Tests Act allowed men of any religion, or of none, to hold office in universities; and Edward Cardwell, the Secretary for War, started to carry out his great series of reforms to modernize the army. The purchase of commissions was abolished; county regiments were formed; troops were issued with a modern breech-loading rifle; flogging was abolished as a punishment in peace-time; and a new short-service engagement of six years was introduced. Shortly afterwards, the navy got its first turret warship, the *Devastation*.

Bribery and corruption in elections was made almost impossible by the Ballot Act of 1872, which fulfilled one of the original Chartist demands by making the vote secret; previously, electors had had to call out the name of their chosen candidate in public. In the same year, the Public Health Act, established sanitary authorities in all parts of the country and made the appointment of a medical officer of health compulsory. (The first, Dr William Duncan, had been appointed in Liverpool under a special Act of Parliament in 1847.) The opening hours of public houses were restricted by the Licensing Act of 1872, which forced them to close on Sunday afternoons and made them shut at 11 pm on weekdays in the provinces and at midnight in London. Habitual 'lushes', however, were not too seriously affected as pubs were allowed to open at 6 am in the provinces and at 5 am in London!

Punch, and many of its readers, did not welcome some of these reforms, even though most of them were both very necessary and long overdue. It was opposed even to the simple justice of allowing women to retain their own earnings: 'the marriage service says

Girl-graduates' tea-parties were not much fun for male chauvinist pigs who would have preferred something stronger (1873)

something about a mystical union, the conditions whereof may not seem exactly satisfied by rival banking accounts.' Punch remained almost as strongly anti-feminist as it had always been. Although it now gave unqualified support to women nurses and doctors and somewhat more qualified approval to the idea of women lawyers, it mocked higher education for women as facetiously as it had done

thirty years before. Girton College was opened at Cambridge in 1873, though its students were not granted the privilege of receiving Cambridge degrees until 1921, and the college was not given full university status until after the Second World War! Punch wrote its own male chauvinist version of the college rules to celebrate the opening, stipulating that there should be no excessive piano-playing; 'a regular supply of sound and wholesome light literature', with copies of *Le Follet* and other fashion journals in the college library; and advice from the sub-mistress and tutors on the fancy-work students might do in their own time. There was to be a Professor of Costume, with an inaugural lecture on 'Winter Fashions' and chairs also in needlework, domestic economy and hygiene, plus a Reader in Etiquette and a Teacher of Darning who would hold evening classes twice a week.

Punch was just as strongly opposed to women's suffrage as it was to women's higher education. A few years before, the philosopher, John Stuart Mill, had introduced a motion in the House of Commons—the first ever of its kind—to give women the vote, but it was defeated by 196 votes to 73. Punch failed to realize that if women did gain the vote they might prefer a female candidate to a man: 'The Ladies' man will gain the day at each election' and 'in their choosing a Member to vote for them in Parliament, the Eyes will often have it'. On the other hand, it continued to campaign for improvement in the conditions of seamstresses and governesses and also launched at this time a new crusade in support of battered wives, by suggesting that wife-beaters should be given a taste of the garotter's medicine, which had by now become something of a panacea. It was baffled and offended that some women were not completely satisfied by its support for such causes, and its own unstinted adoration for conventional members of the fair sex, a form of masculine conceit which was even more difficult to combat than the total opposition of the misogynist. A number of Victorian intellectuals, such as John Ruskin, shared similar attitudes.

Punch was just as critical of the new Licensing Act, which had been passed to please Gladstone's non-conformist supporters. Although Mr Punch loathed monstrous gin-palaces, where a glass of 'Old Tom' could be bought for twopence, and low 'crime-breeding' public houses, he liked a glass or two himself and enjoyed the sight of occasional inebriation among beer-swilling cabbies, with their red noses and their pot bellies, and among languid swells with their unsteady gait and slurred speech: the inalienable right of free-born Britons to choose their own form of enjoyment. He detected a snobbish ambiguity in the strictures of the United Kingdom Alliance, and other temperance societies, which were never directed against 'the nobility and gentry of England' but against the classes 'of whom it demands protection from themselves, to the molestation of others'. Mr Punch could not bear this sanctimonious interference with other people's liberties, and foresaw that if it continued without protest, 'John Bull' would

One of the 'terrible results of the higher education of women' was that they preferred rational conversations with ancient professors to the charming inanities of the young swells who were transformed into wallflowers at receptions (1874)

eventually be transformed into 'John Ox'. He welcomed the decision of the Commissioner of Metropolitan Police to use his discretionary powers to allow taverns near theatres in the West End to stay open until 1 am on weekdays, and the decision of the mayor and magistrates of Oxford, after the receipt of a number of petitions, to allow public houses in the town to stay open until 11.30 pm on weekdays. He hoped that similar petitions elsewhere

THE PROSPECTS OF THE POPPY

So, the Indian revenue comes short by £400,000 in consequence of a fall in the price of opium! How is the depreciation which has befallen that narcotic to be accounted for? Very likely it has been caused by the decline of Mahometanism, whence Mussulmans may have extensively abjured opium together with thin potations, and addicted themselves to beer, and other generous liquors, instead of it. But the opium growers, and the Indian government need not altogether despond. If the United Kingdom Alliance succeed in destroying the British liquor-trade, the consequence of their triumph will in all probability be an immensely increased consumption of opium in the United Kingdom. When exhilarating beverages shall have been banished from the Christmas banquet of the future, people who have eaten as much roast beef and plum-pudding as they can, will then sit after dinner opium-eating, or drinking laudanum. But will not black drop be even worse than blue ruin?

1870

would soon bring other magistrates to their senses. His views reflected a growing feeling among the middle classes, that the government was depriving Englishmen of their hard-won freedom:

> By Liberal rulers so governed are we
> That year after year we get less and less free;
> And feel, though we try hard the feeling to smother,
> That Liberty's one thing, and Licence another.

Gladstone himself admitted after his electoral defeat in 1874 that he had been 'borne down in a torrent of gin and beer'.

Who were these Victorian middle classes? As even a cursory glance at the pages of any volume of Punch will show, they were never a homogenous, united or static group of people. They included at the one extreme, 'the modern money makers', the cotton spinners and brokers, the brewers, the ironmasters and the engineers, the 'new landed interest', who, with their ducal incomes of £10,000 or more a year, had already dispossessed some of the old aristocracy and were living in splendour on their estates; and at the other, the government clerk trying to bring up a family and to keep up appearances on an income of £200 a year and the underpaid curate in search of a better living for the future or an advantageous match in his present parish. They were swept up in the whirlwind of ambition towards the glittering prizes which seemed to be within the grasp of any man who was possessed of native energy and acquired skills. The Victorian age was never safe and secure, though the ladies frustrated in opportunities for sexual enjoyment, higher education and useful employment, might try to make it so; it was restless, relentless and cruel, an unending struggle in which only the fittest could survive. The men were as restless as the age in which they lived, involved in a fight to keep

Sunday opening was strongly opposed: here the alternative to the public house is seen as the house of education for the public (1869)

up appearances, to make more money, and, often, to escape from their origins, which could be easily revealed by some solecism on the hunting field or at the dining table.

Hospitable Host: Does any gentleman say pudden?

Precise Guest: No, sir. No *gentleman* says *pudden*.

To become a member of the middle classes was more a matter of aspirations and aspirates than of income, though there was a financial dividing line of about £150 to £200 a year, distinguishing those who could afford to employ a solitary maid-of-all-work from those who could not.

These men—and their wives, their children, and their servants—are all to be found in the pages of Punch, the wealthy, and sometimes illiterate, manufacturers, the speculators, the city men, the lawyers, the farmers, the clergymen, the curates, the school inspectors and the university dons. They were joined at the beginning of the 1870s by representatives of the increasing columns of book-keepers and clerks in banks, law firms and city offices, who could now more easily afford to buy newspapers and magazines whose prices had been reduced by the repeal of the paper duty in 1861, the last of the Taxes on Knowledge. The white collar passion for words was noted in 1871. 'Whatever educationists may say upon the matter, there is little doubt, we fancy, that there is a growing taste for literature among our humbler classes. Look at the daily crowd gathered round the *Punch*

'What we may expect to see this season.' The velocipede, an early form of bicycle, attracted great interest among both men and women, though the latter, for reasons of decency, had to learn to ride side-saddle (1869)

window! See the clusters studying the placards of the newspapers.' The first editor, Mark Lemon, had died on May 23, 1870. His successor, Shirley Brooks, extended the vision of the magazine to include country rustics, Scottish shepherds, and the lower middle classes, who were just moving out of the cities at that time to new, and often jerry-built, semi-detached houses in the inner suburbs, where they commuted daily by steam train; but it was not until 1888, after the Education Act of 1870 had produced a whole new generation of literates, that Punch published in serial form that classic saga of lower middle-class life, *The Diary of a Nobody*.

The lower-middle classes started to move out to new terraced houses in the suburbs in the 1870s, even though it meant the sea-side holiday had to be sacrificed. But as paterfamilias explains to his wife, 'who could want a change of air when they had such a delightful garden as this' (1871)

Before the turn of the century, the same factors had produced in a different publishing sphere *Tit-bits* and the *Daily Mail*.

It is during this period—much earlier than most people imagine—that we hear the first sustained squeals of protest and groans of oppression of a modern kind from the middle classes. Outwardly, many of them seemed to be as firmly established and as entrenched as ever, with their hordes of servants, their huge mansions, and their eight-course dinner parties. Fashions had become more volatile and revealing but no less expensive. The crinoline had been replaced by the bustle; skirts were either very long, or short enough to reveal a daring ankle; the neckline

---

THE SCOTTISH SCENE

English Tourist (having arrived at Greenock on Sunday morning): My man, what's your charge for rowing me across the Firth?
Boatman: Weel, Sir, I was just thinkin', I canna break the Sawbath-Day for no less than f'fteen shull'n's!!

Tourist: Your dog appears to be deaf, as he pays no attention to me.
Shepherd: Na, na, Sir. She's a varra wise dog for all tat. But she only speaks Gaelic.

1873

PROSPERITY AND PROGRESS

Oysters are going,
Salmon is growing
Scarcer and scarcer, boys, year after year;
Mouths must be shut on
Beef, veal and mutton,
Butcher's meat got so confoundedly dear.

Prices for chicken
Poulterers stick in;
Fowls are about twice as dear as they were.
Splendidly living
People are giving
Six, seven, eight and nine shillings a pair.

House-rent is rising.
Very surprising!
Births still increase at a wonderful rate,
O the severity
Of our prosperity!
Hey! Will Posterity want or abate?

1869

dropped for a time to a point 'so low as to be barely decent', which, in Victorian times, meant that it exposed the shoulders and the throat; and there was a fashion for wearing coquettish Dolly Varden clothes, named after the character in *Barnaby Rudge*, consisting of large hats abundantly trimmed with flowers and print dresses with large floral patterns. There was a growing interest in that new form of transport, the velocipede, an early form of the bicycle, and, among the wealthy, a nostalgic revival of the coach and four-in-hand, equivalent to the preservation of steam locomotives and veteran cars today. *Bézique* had become a fashionable card game; the middle classes were collecting more antiques; and Chinamania, which had started in the late 1850s, had become even more frenetic.

But many members of the middle classes felt that their own living standards were being eroded by rising prices, increased duties and taxes, and static salaries. In the public sector, many clerks found it particularly difficult to keep up appearances on their small annual salaries of £100 or £200, while others, in the cause of retrenchment, which was 'now the order of the day', were dismissed after many years of service, without a penny piece of compensation. Stipendiary magistrates in London were much more highly paid, but even they found it more difficult to maintain their traditional way of life, as they had not had a pay-rise for thirty-five years! Their £1,200 a year bought less and less in a period of rapidly rising prices. Punch estimated in 1869 that the 'cost of living has of late been nearly doubled' which may have been something of an exaggeration, as some historians calculate that prices rose by only 50 per cent or so between 1850 and 1873, the increase being particularly great in the last few years of that period. Even if their calculations are right, and we all know how false even contemporary statistics can be, the feelings of the people who were living at the time were often quite despairing. Home-produced meat had become so expensive that many of the working classes, and some of the middle classes, could no longer afford to buy it:

> Once mighty roast beef was the Englishman's food
> It has now grown so dear that 'tis nearly tabooed.

There were lurking anxieties then, as there are today, that supplies of fossil fuels would become exhausted. A cartoon of 1868 shows an old gentleman sitting in front of a fire and saying to his maid: 'Pray, don't put too many coals on, Mary! It makes me shiver when I think that in three hundred years we shall have none left.'

It was not this potential shortage, however, which caused a massive increase in the price of household fuel at that time, but strikes, lock-outs and excessive exports. In some districts the price went up by 40 per cent in a single year, contributing to the increase of deaths from hypothermia in the particularly severe winter of 1873. Property prices went up, too—a small city tavern was sold for over £20,000, or £20 a square foot, in 1872—and although many of the middle classes only rented or leased their homes (as the new permanent building societies catered mainly for the working classes and not for them), they were affected by the increase in the rents of villas and mansions. The legacy duty, which had been extended in 1853, after much controversy, from personal possessions to real estate, was also increased.

The main grievance of the middle classes was the income tax, which had been reintroduced by Peel as a temporary expedient for three years in 1842, and still had not been abolished thirty years later, demonstrating that the value of ministerial promises then was no higher than it often is today. The rate of income tax, by modern penal standards, was minute: it was actually reduced to only threepence in the £ in 1873. But it was not so much the level, as the 'partiality' of the tax which infuriated the middle classes, as it was not usually collected on wages, but only on income from land, houses, farming, government stock, trades, professions and on salaries and pensions in the public sector. As a result, a government clerk had to pay income tax on his quarterly salary, while a manual worker who might be earning more in some industries, such as engineering and mining, paid nothing. The cost of reforms, such as the abolition of the purchase of army commissions, came directly out of the pockets of the middle classes, as the income tax was raised from fourpence to sixpence in the £ to pay for it. The 'perfectly unjust' incidence of taxation caused the middle classes to hold protest meetings in Birmingham and in London, where the formation of an Anti-Income Tax League was mooted. Punch declared in 1871, though the words might have been written yesterday: 'If you don't want your incomes exceptionally taxed, don't make money otherwise than by manual labour: and if you don't want your children or your brothers and sisters to be fined for the public benefit, on the amount you may leave, don't put any by.' Two years later, under the heading, *Plunder for the People*, Punch quoted approvingly the following extract from the *Morning Post*:

> In the reduction of taxation, the Working Classes have been the principal gainers. To exempt them from imposts which they are well able to bear, the Income-tax has been retained upon the class immediately above them, whose circumstances are not by any means so prosperous, and who have not been able to enforce a higher payment for their services to meet the increased cost of living.

In reality, the middle classes do not seem to have had very much to grumble about. A series of calculations made by one statistician in 1869 showed that the eight million men, women and children, who constituted the middle classes, shared a gross annual income of £490 million on which they paid a total of £54 million in taxes, direct and indirect; while the twenty-two million workers had an aggregate income of only £325 million, on which they paid £29 million in taxes. Perhaps it was simply that the middle classes even then had felt the way the wind was blowing and did not appreciate this first slight chill.

Nevertheless, 'poor paterfamilias' certainly felt that he had far more troubles to contend with. Some of the younger wives, with their Dolly Varden clothes and their pert remarks were becoming a little too emancipated, if not downright improper:

Lady: Oh, Mr. Mastic, why do artists have screens about their studio?

Artist: To back up the figures, and so on.

Lady: Oh, really! Well I thought it was to keep the bedstead and all that out of sight!

Some of their daughters, with their desire for education and the vote, and their off-the-shoulder dresses, were little better:

Aunt (slightly shocked): Why, child, all your clothes are falling off.

Laura: Oh, dear no, Aunty. It's the fashion!

Sons were also becoming far too improvident.

Sister: I say, Bob that looks like a tailor's bill.

Bob: Yes—just fancy! I have let that fellow dress me as he likes for the last three years, and now he has the impudence to send me his bill!

After a hard day's work, paterfamilias came home not to peace and contentment, but to his son's bills, his daughter's demands, and his wife's complaints about the servants, who were becoming more impudent every year. Servants seemed to have lost all respect for their betters:

Opposite: *My Lady:* 'And why did you leave your last situation?' *Sensitive being:* '*Well*, my lady, I 'adn't been in the 'ouse 'ardly a month when I hascertained as the ladies of the family 'ad never even been presented at court!' (1873)

Above right: *Young Swell:* 'We won't go down Conduit Street, for I haven't paid my tailor his Christmas bill yet, and if he should see me he might feel embarrassed!' (1869)

Young mistress: Jane, I'm surprised that none of you stood up when I went into the kitchen just now.

Jane: Indeed, Mum! which we was surprised ourselves at you a comin' into the kitching while we was a 'aving our luncheong!! Soon, ladies would be expected to produce a letter of recommendation when engaging an under kitchen-maid; all housemaids would have the right to use the piano and to have a weekly singing lesson free of charge; and an upper servants' ball would have to be given at least once a month.

Tradesmen, those 'rascals' and 'cheats', were just as bad as the servants, with whom they were usually in league. It was well known that cooks demanded a percentage from the tradesmen whom they favoured with their orders, and that this commission had eventually to come out of the mistress's housekeeping money through artificially inflated prices. Shopkeepers were dishonest in other ways. They gave short measure; and many of their goods were inferior or adulterated. Tea was popularly known as 'sloe

An early middle-class victim of 'nervous depression' tries to banish his anxiety by spending six weeks alone in the country, without tobacco or drink (1869)

poison' after one of the means of adulteration which was used; another was chopped hay. Sand was mixed with sugar; chicory, beans and even bones, were added to ground coffee; alum was used in the making of bread; plaster of Paris was added to confectionery; pig's lard was mixed in with butter; mutton pies were made from cat; strychnine, salts and water were added to beer; and milk was adulterated with chalk. To stop these, and similar dishonest practices, the first 'clean food' law was passed in 1872— the Adulteration of Food, Drinks and Drugs Act— which made it illegal to add other ingredients to foodstuffs to increase their weight.

To counter rising prices, the middle classes started to use the same weapon which had been introduced among the working classes in 1844, when some hand-loom weavers set up the first co-operative society shop in Rochdale. The co-operative movement had spread so rapidly among the working classes that by 1850 there were about one hundred and thirty similar stores and by 1875 well over a thousand. The first middle-class co-operative, the Civil Service Supply Association, which had been formed by Post Office clerks to provide cheaper tea, opened a store in the Strand in 1868; four years later, the Army and Navy Stores was opened in Victoria Street, originally to supply wine at a discount to officers and their families. Both co-operatives had a phenomenal success and rapidly

NO END OF STRIKES

A strike, my Masters, and my Men, is a game at which not only two can play, but likewise three. Besides the Workman and the Employer, who strikes by locking-out, there is the Consumer, whose strike consists in going without. He goes without that which he can least inconveniently do without: thus a man redresses the balance of his butcher's bill by striking, if a bachelor, against his tailor; if a husband, against his linen-draper, as much as possible, against his jeweller altogether. Accordingly, Trades-Unionists of all sorts, please to observe, that one trade eventually suffers for the strike of another; and that, in so far as you are consumers, when you strike as producers you may strike against yourselves, and oblige yourselves to strike again by-and-by against some one particular class of producers or other. Then these or those, in their turn, strike against you, and thus of striking there is no end.

1872

introduced many other kinds of goods into their stores. Other co-operatives were formed. One cartoon of 1868 shows Florence, a dim brunette, arousing her somnolent husband with the words: 'Gus, dear, wake up. I've had a brilliant idea! We save five per cent, you know, by belonging to a co-operative society; but suppose we belong to *two* societies, we shall save *ten* per cent.' Co-operatives gradually opened their doors to all middle-class customers, regardless of their employment or rank, and other firms, many of them long-established, were forced to offer discounts to co-operative members or to slash prices.

The effort to keep the wolf from the door (which becomes quite a common phrase in Punch at this time), the increasing expense of keeping a wife and family, the greater strains and stresses in working life (and over-indulgence in food and drink), were already starting to take their toll among middle-class men. In 1872, Punch republished some statistics from the *British Medical Journal*, showing that death from heart disease among men between twenty and forty-five years of age had increased by 22 per cent in the previous twenty years.

The middle classes had no doubts about the causes of their present discontents. They blamed agitators like George Odger, a shoemaker by trade, who fomented trouble among the 'idiotic portion of the London mob' by addressing 'nuisance meetings' in Trafalgar Square demanding revolution and a republic. They blamed the increasing powers of the unions, banded together in the Trades Union Congress since 1868, which were the only organizations in the land of free trade who could interfere with 'the operation of natural laws regulating supply and demand'. They blamed the government which robbed 'the few and the weak to curry favour with the many and the strong'. As a consequence, workmen had become emancipated from 'all restraint' and could dictate 'their own terms without regard to the consequences on other people.'

In the early 1870s the country was engulfed by a wave of strikes, which continued even after the Criminal Law Amendment Act of 1871 had made picketing illegal. The gas stokers in London stopped work, hoping to plunge the capital into darkness; the police went on strike; the bakers came out; and even poor Hodge laid down his tools when Joseph Arch organized the first successful widespread stoppage of work among farm labourers. Employers retaliated by locking out workers; farmers also evicted many of their labourers from tied cottages. Punch had to admit that some of these strikes were justified. It had not forsaken all its sympathy for the exploited farm workers, some of whom succeeded only in increasing their pittance of eight shillings a week by a miserable shilling; and it agreed that the journeymen bakers of London, who endured 'more than ordinarily penal labour' had a very reasonable case, as they were demanding no increase in pay but merely that their hours of work should be reduced from eighteen to twelve consecutive hours a day! But the aggregate effect of these strikes was to push up working-class wages, and prices.

The real obloquy was reserved for one special class of workers, the miners. The coal-mining industry was expanding rapidly at this time and continued to do so as a general trend until the First World War when a peak production of 287 million tons a year was reached. There were strikes, and lock-outs in many mining areas, as colliers demanded higher wages for their arduous, dangerous and unhealthy work underground. By working-class standards some of them were already earning high wages of £234 a year or more, which was more than the salary of many a lower middle-class clerk. Their prosperity, however, was greatly exaggerated by the middle classes. When an official Inspector of Mines for Lancashire agreed at an inquiry in 1873 that miners did occasionally indulge in the luxury of drinking champagne, his belief was rapidly transformed into firm conviction and finally into established fact, with miners all over the country quaffing draughts of champagne and eating meat—which other people could not afford to buy— four times a day. Punch had great fun with the affluence of miners. A cartoon of 1873 showed a lady and a pitman in a greengrocers:

My Lady: I'm afraid I must give up the pineapple, Mr Green! Eight shillings is really too much!

Successful collier: Just put 'un up for me, then, master. 'Ere's 'arf a sovereign; and look 'ere—yer may keep the change if yer'll only tell us 'ow to cook 'un.

Miners were portrayed as gamekeepers protecting their colleagues' shooting preserves; and when it was rumoured that some colliers were riding to work on horseback, the comment was: 'We shall soon, perhaps, hear that these industrious, hard-working fellows are keeping their carriages as well as their horses.' It was pointed out that a miner had an unfair advantage over a middle-class man as he had no appearances to keep up in the pit. He could 'inhabit any hovel' and go about in 'patched clothes and boots'. If miners continued to secure such large pay increases by striking, 'our masters, the colliers will by-and-by, perhaps, have succeeded in extorting from their employers above a whole week's wages for half a day's work'. The liberal professions would be entered only by those who were born as millionaires and any boy who was not born with a silver spoon in his mouth would go into the 'liberally remunerated' profession of mining.

Workers who did not represent a competitive threat, to the purchasing power of the middle classes still received some consolation and sympathy in their distress so long as they were deserving cases. Poverty had coagulated into hard clots in the dingy alleyways and airless courts of the capital, as unskilled workers were increasingly deprived of the chance of making a better living by unscrupulous employers and by trade unions which, in the main, deliberately excluded them from membership.

WORKHOUSE CURIOSITIES

At a Conversazione of the Poor Law Commissioners, the following curiosities were the other evening shown . . .

Photograph of a Poor-law Inspector, as he appears when 'inspecting' a workhouse with his eyes shut.

Model of the 'rabbit-hutch' which the Farnham Guardians considered in cold blood to be 'quite good enough for tramps'.

A pair of damp sheets from a poorhouse infirmary.

A bit of one of the hot bricks by which a girl was scorched severely, and was so weakminded as to die in consequence.

Samples of workhouse wine in various stages of emaciation, showing its increasing weakness in every hand through which it passes, from the master of the workhouse down to the pauper nurse, until at length it reaches the poor patient for whom it is prescribed.

Specimens of an infirmary blanket, warranted not to keep the cold out.

A slice of pauper Christmas pudding, curious as showing how much pudding can be made with how few plums.

One of the toys broken by the order of a master of a workhouse, in order that the children might not be too happy there.

Sketch (coloured) of the cesspool into which the epileptic Farnham pauper fell perversely, and so died.

A specimen of hard, tough beef, administered to toothless paupers, when they are ordered by the doctor a tender mutton-chop.

A bottle of air taken from a workhouse bedroom. In proof of its impurity, a light being placed in it immediately goes out.

One of the newspapers removed by the late Master at Farnham, who feared that the paupers might really be too comfortable. . . .

1868

'Oh, look here, Mr Crispin! I bought these boots here only a week ago, and they're beginning to crack already!'

'Ah, miss! Perhaps you've been *walking* in them! *Our* boots are intended for *carriage people*, you know!' (1873)

In 1868 it was noted that pauperism in London had increased by 50 per cent in the previous three years, rising from 100,000 to 150,000. There were also another 100,000 children without proper guardianship, food or education. A 'vast deal' of the poverty arose from 'the saddest of causes—want of work, where there is willingness to work'. The wards of the huge, barracks-like workhouses were 'crammed to suffocation' with the 'casual crowding of naked human beings in sties, where their humanity is speedily effaced', and where fever and disease were rampant. The old English vice of bumbledom was to blame, the 'penny wisdom and pound folly' of small shopkeepers, 'not usually gifted with

large minds', who now controlled many of the Boards of Guardians.

Many contemporary writers noted the increasing poverty of the East End at this time. Some of the public amenities which had been introduced in the previous decade were now in decay for want of subscriptions, like the Model Baths in Goulston Square, Whitechapel, which had been opened by Prince Albert. In 1872, some of South Kensington's 'superfluous light' was radiated into 'the outer darkness of East London' by opening a branch of the Victoria and Albert Museum in Bethnal Green, which did not close its doors until ten at night 'to fight the gin-shop and the tap-room on fair terms'.

Another cause of poverty was the population explosion. The total number of people in the United Kingdom had increased from 26,751,000 in 1841 to 31,556,000 in 1871. The population continued to increase at an alarming rate of 1,173 a day (a net increase of 705 a day after emigration) as 'birth control' still remained dirty words even among the middle classes and natural methods of withdrawal were rarely practised by the working classes. (Charles Bradlaugh and Annie Besant were both heavily fined in 1877 for republishing an American booklet on birth control.) It would have been far better to have a stationary population like France, Punch declared in 1871, but 'gregarious opinion compels you, on the contrary to extol the continued numerical progress, and the railway-paced advancement in manufacturing industry of this great commercial nation'.

But population control could not be an election issue then. In his campaign at the beginning of 1874, Gladstone promised another education act, university reform, better local government in London, 'a free breakfast table' by ending duties on tea, coffee and sugar, and the total abolition of the income tax. But his promises came too late to placate those voters whom he had offended by his reforms. He suffered an overwhelming defeat at the hands of the Conservatives, who gained a clear working majority for the first time since 1841. In March 1874, Disraeli became prime minister, and introduced a very different style of government.

6 DIZZY GLITTER

1874–1880

From the mid-1870s, middle-class existence began to undergo a fundamental change. Oh, by latter-day standards and even more in comparison with the blighted, barren lives of the working classes of those times, the middle classes still lived in incredible splendour and luxury, with their maids at £20 or so a year, and a governess or a plain cook at not much more; with sugar at twopence a pound; oysters at a shilling a dozen, or as little as fourpence from a market stall; whisky at three shillings a bottle; and seven-course dinners in reasonable London restaurants for half a crown. Income tax had reached its lowest-ever point of twopence in the £ in 1874, and although it was doubled four years later that still represented a rate of only 1.6 per cent. Substantial houses with four or five bedrooms and attics for the maids were freely available in town and in the country, at low rents. Foreign travel had become even more popular: whirlwind package tours, organized by Thomas Cook, cost as little as £10 a head.

Brown Senior: Well, Fred, what did you see during your trip abroad?

Brown Junior: Aw, 'pon m' word. Don't know what I saw 'xactly, only know I did more by three countries, eight towns and four mountains, than Smith did in the same time!

Women had ample time, and opportunity, for recreation with tennis parties on the smooth home lawns, cut now by hand lawn-mowers pushed by the family gardener; and in winter there was tobogganing on the snowy slopes of Hampstead Heath. Pet dogs were as extreme as the fashions, which changed with bewildering speed during these few years, from the bunched-up bustle to the sheath skirt, which was so tight that ladies were unable to bend, and from the frilly, pinafore frock to the long belted jacket and barely flared skirt, which gave a masculine outline. Indoors, there seemed to be as many dinner parties and musical soirées as there had ever been, and a new 'toy', developed by the American, Thomas Edison, in 1877:

Mistress: You needn't be so frightened, Maria. It's only the phonograph.

Maria: Lor, Mum! I thought it was a sewing machine. And I only just touched the handle, and it spoke just like the very moral of master.

But the world-wide Great Depression, which had started in 1873, cast long shadows, which were to coalesce into even more

Previous pages: Hub of a rapidly-growing empire; the Pool of London in the 1870s.

Above: Emancipated young ladies, watched by their idle admirers, play tennis in their long dresses and hats (1874)

frightening shapes and spectres in the 1880s, over the fortunes and the future of the middle classes. British exports increased in volume, but not in money value owing to the decline in world prices. British farmers, in particular, and some manufacturers were undercut by overseas rivals. There was much unemployment which rose at times to an estimated 10 per cent or more of the working population.

Although many different members of the middle classes were affected, it was the farmer who was most severely beset. Ironically, Disraeli, who had unsuccessfully fought Peel thirty years earlier to retain agricultural protection, presided over this disastrous slump in traditional British farming, as free trade, and the construction of railroads across the vast plains of Canada and the

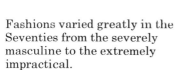

Fashions varied greatly in the Seventies from the severely masculine to the extremely impractical.

Top: 'The levelling tendency of modern dress.' The old gentleman suggests that the verger should tell 'those youths' to take their hats off, only to discover that they are 'the dean's young ladies' (1876)

Right: Neither the lady nor her escort are able to bend down to retrieve her handkerchief! (1878)

Opposite: Cheap meat from the United States brought disaster to many British farmers during the agricultural depression (1876)

Above: The financial plight of the middle classes became so acute in their own eyes, that Punch envisaged children parading the streets in an attempt to let the family home so that they could have a summer holiday (1876)

United States, allowed cheap wheat, harvested from the virgin soil by mechanical reaper, to be sent to east-coast ports for transhipment to Britain. The United States and Australia also started to export cheap canned meat to Britain around this time. To add to the British farmers' troubles, there were bad harvests in 1877, 1878 and 1879, the last being particularly disastrous owing to prolonged rain during the harvest. Many farmers, particularly those who grew cereals, went bankrupt or left the land. A cartoon of 1879 shows a landlord talking to a tenant farmer who has quit at the end of his lease to await better times:

Landlord: Well, Jackson, how do you like living on your capital?
Farmer: Not too well, my lord: but I find it cheaper than letting you live on it!

The total acreage of arable land was reduced by a quarter and the acreage of wheat was halved, as farmers were forced to turn increasingly to dairy farming and the cultivation of fruit and vegetables for the expanding towns.

Manufacturers also shivered in the chill economic wind as tariff barriers were erected in many other countries, making it more difficult for them to export. Financiers and investors were affected by the general lack of international confidence; the failure of banks in Vienna in 1873 and in Paris nine years later; defaults by foreign debtors; and rapidly declining dividends from their overseas holdings:

First City Man (Optimist): How's business with you? I can't help thinking things are bet——

Second City Man (Pessimist): Drifting fast to the workhouse! And what makes me doubly anxious is I can't think who'll be left to pay the poor-rate!

Punch advised bank depositors to marry a daughter to an influential bank director. 'Then while there is yet time, and they are off their guard, sell your shares and withdraw your deposits. This is the only safe way of investing in a Joint Stock Bank.' Investors in railways were advised to live on the line and to count the rolling stock daily, while 'if your property is a Mine, *live at the bottom, and never leave it.'* Middle-class sons were also affected by the 'over-crowded avenues to employment', which had been further restricted, by competitive examinations, so that 'hard-up' became the new motto of 'many an elegant young gentleman not born to fortune'. Punch, under its new editor, Tom Taylor, who had succeeded Shirley Brooks in 1874, tried to get what fun it could out of the depression:

George, dear, don't you think it is rather *extravagant* of you to eat butter with that delicious jam?

No, love—*economical.* Same piece of bread does for both!

But in those trying times, the middle-class sense of humour had begun to wear a little thin.

THE THREE R'S AND THE RATEPAYERS

(A Parochial Poem)

O School-board, whose administration
Provides compulsory education
For children of the needy Masses,
Called, saucily, the Lower Classes,
Which schooling, my but too dear Board,
We Ratepayers must perforce afford
To youth whom better-nurtured lads
And lasses would describe as 'Cads';
Let them be taught their hands to use
To polish plate, clean boots and shoes;
To mend and darn, to cook and sew—
All things they chiefly need to know:
Such industries as those must learn
Who'll early have their bread to earn.
Then next imbue their minds with letters,
So much in common with their betters,
As, crammed at costlier schools in vain,
Most of those better e'er retain.
Teach all their R's—that primal Three!
But 'ware the letters L.S.D.,
Nor give, at our cost, education
That may unfit folks for their station.

1879

By the time the Great Depression finally ended in 1896, the English middle classes emerged from the shadows into a new world which had changed beyond recall. Great Britain was still great—immensely great by present-day standards—but it had lost for ever its unique position as the workshop of the world, the fundamental basis of former middle-class predominance and prosperity, and would have to live in competition with other powerful nations such as the United States and Germany, who had already surpassed Britain in steel production, and were more advanced in some of the new growth sectors, such as the chemical, electrical and machine tools industries. The middle classes had also lost their assured position at home through increasing intervention by the government in the economy, and the inexorable progress of the trade unions, which had now fully emerged from their long period of relative quiescence. Some of the middle classes had lost their old sense of adventure and their vigour. The possibilities of rising quickly in society as a free individual or as an *entrepreneur* were still very much greater than they are today, but they were already decreasing and, as time passed, they were to become even less. It was the colonies which were to present more opportunities of that kind in the future. During the Great Depression, the cost of living had fallen by an estimated 33 per cent, which was of greatest benefit to the wage-earner and those on the lowest salaries; but the richer members of the middle classes had to cope with higher income tax, increases in rates and the new estate duties which were introduced by the Liberals in 1894.

It was Benjamin Disraeli, or 'Dizzy' as he was commonly called, the only British prime minister of Jewish ancestry, who, like some latter-day Old Testament prophet, tried to lead the reluctant middle classes out of the slough of depression into new paths of imperial glory. There has never been another prime minister like him, before or since: a great orator; a sparkling wit and brilliant *raconteur*; an accomplished novelist and a much better letter-writer; a political and social adventurer; a dandy who dyed his hair and rouged his cheeks in old age; an opportunist and a flatterer, particularly of women; a husband who married for money and learnt to love his wife; a spendthrift; and a man of Oriental vision.

Disraeli's ministry was responsible for a number of important reforms, including the Artisans' and Labourers' Dwellings Improvement Act which gave local councils powers of compulsory purchase for slum clearance; a Public Health Act, parts of which are still in force to this day; and the Conspiracy and Protection of Property Act, which legalized peaceful picketing again and prevented workers from being prosecuted for conspiracy merely for taking part in a strike. These Acts, however, were all the work of the Home Secretary, Viscount Cross; Disraeli's vision, despite myopia, was focused on far distant places.

In 1875, Disraeli brought off a great personal coup by borrowing £4 million from the banking house of Rothschild while parliament

was in recess, to buy a large minority stake for Britain in the Suez Canal from the bankrupt Khedive of Egypt, shares which might otherwise have been purchased by France to give it sole control over that important sea link. In 1875, the Prince of Wales made a spectacular tour of India and in the following year Disraeli introduced an Act making Queen Victoria the Empress of India.

He was also preoccupied with the Eastern Question at this time. After a revolt in their province of Bulgaria, the Turks had massacred twelve thousand men, women and children. Russia again intervened, as it had done during the Crimean War, and made some gains of territory at the end of its war against Turkey. Disraeli succeeded in reducing some of these gains at the Congress of Berlin, held in 1878 under the chairmanship of 'the honest broker', Bismarck, and gained for Britain the right to occupy the Turkish island of Cyprus. These gains—the Suez Canal shares and Cyprus—forged new links in the vital life-line to India, which had been started with the acquisition of Gibraltar in 1713, of Malta in 1814, and of Aden in 1839.

The Queen, a widow still living in mourning, was as delighted by Disraeli's cleverness as she was by his constant flattery of her; while Disraeli, who was also a widower by this time, was gratified to be on such intimate terms of affection with his sovereign. Their relationship became something of a mutual admiration society. Disraeli's private nickname for the Queen was 'the Faery', from Spenser's *Faery Queen*. In a letter to the Countess of Bradford after the purchase of the Suez Canal shares, Disraeli wrote: 'The Faery is in ecstasies about "this great and important event".' The Queen confessed in her private journal that she was 'all for the Titles Bill', which made her the Empress of India, and after it was passed, she rewarded Disraeli by making *him* the Earl of Beaconsfield. She also acknowledged his success in bringing back 'peace with honour' (his own phrase) from the Congress of Berlin by investing him with the Order of the Garter.

But many other people were less dazzled by his achievements. Most of the Cabinet had been sceptical (wrongly) about the purchase of the Suez Canal shares. There had been opposition in parliament—'inexplicable', wrote the Queen in her journal—to the title of Empress of India and as many derogatory remarks about Disraeli's honour. Punch published a cartoon showing the crowned Victoria placing a coronet on the head of the kneeling Disraeli with the title: 'Empress and Earl, or, One Good Turn Deserves Another'. Disraeli's refusal to condemn the Turkish massacres, long after they had been revealed by Gladstone in his famous pamphlet, *The Bulgarian Horrors and the Question of the East*, shocked the conscience of the nation, particularly the non-conformist section; though his blustering policy towards Russia gained him support from the more bellicose sectors of the community. A popular music-hall song of the time, sung by G H MacDermott ran:

Opposite above left: Disraeli's purchase of the Suez Canal shares helped to secure the key to the important sea route to India (1875)

Opposite above right: *Turkey:* 'Will you not still befriend me?' *Britannia:* 'Befriend you? Not with your hands of *that colour*' (1878)

Opposite below: The Prince of Wales on his tour of India (1875)

We don't want to fight, but, by Jingo, if we do,
We've got the ships, we've got the men, we've got the money, too.
We've fought the Bear before,
And while Britons shall be true
The Russians shall not have Constantinople.

The Times also eulogized Disraeli for his 'extraordinary success' at the Congress of Berlin, which was 'one of the most honourable triumphs in the modern diplomacy of England'.

Even though the middle classes were dependent on the colonies in many different ways, they were reluctant initially to follow in Dizzy's footsteps. They needed the colonies as a source of food, raw materials and gold. It was a shortage of the latter item which had helped to cause the Great Depression by restricting the money supply at a time when the gold sovereign was the monetary unit of Great Britain, Germany had just gone on the gold standard, and the United States was about to restore the convertibility of the dollar.

'New crowns for old ones!' In return for his support in making her the Queen of India, Victoria made Disraeli an earl (1876)

India was the prime jewel in the imperial crown. Since the Mutiny it had been ruled by a British viceroy and garrisoned by British troops. It provided employment opportunities for the middle classes in the Indian Civil Service; a valuable export market for capital goods, such as railways, and for consumer goods, such as that staple product, textiles; and an equally profitable export trade of its own to the rest of Asia, particularly in opium.

The white colonies were also increasingly important export markets for capital goods and useful, too, as places of banishment for black sheep of the middle classes, and 'blackguards' of the working classes, as transportation to Western Australia was not finally abolished until 1867. The middle classes tolerated the colonies so long as they provided profits and did not involve the mother country in prolonged and costly wars.

Punch had long held a strong antipathy to the colonies, whether they were white, yellow, black or brown. In 1871, it complained that 'the word "colonies" does not usually suggest fun'. Although with its consistent sense of the newsworthy, it followed Stanley to Africa in his search for David Livingstone and the Prince of Wales on his triumphal procession across India, it failed to come up with anything but the worst kind of facetiousness. It started the tour of Africa, the 'Keep-it-Dark Continent' on the east coast at 'Jarnziri-Bar' where 'most of the lively inhabitants were out practising at the bar' and went on to meet the Emperor Jokki, who was dressed, as you might have guessed, in a jockey's striped jersey and peaked cap. Punch had no greater success in India, 'Injyable Injia', where it encountered Sir Jak Holkar, who was no 'Jokar' because he would insist on wearing a European hat, and, later, 'the Nabobs, the Nobobs and the Hobnobs, all fraternising together'. To its great credit, it did give strong support in 1877 to the fund-raising

The great emperor, Jokki (1878)

'A black "White Elephant".' The eventual capture of the Zulu warrior-king Cetewayo, presented an embarrassing problem for John Bull. It was suggested, rudely, that he might be exhibited in the aquarium (1879)

appeal for the millions who were threatened with starvation in the Madras famine, which had killed half a million people in the first few months. But it was much less sympathetic to the second Afghan War of 1878 to 1879, which was fought to maintain Afghanistan as a buffer state between India and Russia. At the end of the war it commented: 'Peace with honour again! Hooray! Peace with Afghanistan. Not peace at any price. Peace at the price of only sixty thousand a year subsidy to Yakoob Khan.' In truth, it had very little sympathy with the sub-continent. 'What good has England got by India?' it asked in the same year. 'Little more, short-sighted cynics will be apt to say, than gorged livers, grass-widows, chudders, chutney and curry.'

Punch became even more disgruntled during the Zulu War of 1879, which was fought to protect the Boers in the Transvaal from the warrior-king, Cetewayo. 'Of all our Colonies, the Cape is the most plague and the least profit. The Boers of Transvaal provoke the Kaffirs to come down upon them, and then expect us to fight their battles. In short, these confounded Boers are about the greatest bores in being.' The war soon revealed that Cardwell's reforms had produced little immediate impact on the efficiency of the army. Troops under the command of Lord Chelmsford marched into Zululand, but their base camp at Isandhlwana was overrun in a surprise attack and five hundred British troops were slaughtered. Lord Chelmsford was also credited by Punch with losing the baggage train of a whole division. This initial humiliation was only redeemed when a small force of troops under the command of two lieutenants 'saved not only a colony, but the credit of Old England' by their heroic defence of Rorke's drift on the River Tulega. Using flour bags and biscuit tins as parapets, they prevented the Zulu warriors from invading Natal. Eventually, ten thousand reinforcements, including the Marines, had to be sent from England under the command of Sir Garnet Wolseley, to ensure success, which came with the capture of Cetewayo, 'the fattest savage south the Equator' in July 1879.

The war, Punch declared, had been both unnecessary and 'one of the costliest blunders of modern times'. John Bull would have to find yet another £10 million to pay for Disraeli's 'glitter':

> For his games with the Afghan, the Zulu, the Turk
> I've to find the hard tin, and it's jolly hard work.

Disraeli's attempt to revive the spirit of imperialism had come to initial grief at Isandhlwana, and at Kabul in Afghanistan. Gladstone made these disasters the main theme of his election addresses during the first Midlothian campaign and won an overwhelming victory over Disraeli in April 1880.

But, through chance or foresight, Disraeli had opened up new paths of hope and glory for England at the beginning of its long, slow century of relative decline. He had demonstrated that if colonies could not provide fun, they could at least produce romance and splendour, themes which were to be developed later by such practical visionaries as Cecil Rhodes and by such writers as Rudyard Kipling and Rider Haggard. The Empire was to become even more vital in the following decades as Britain, weakened relatively by the increasing economic strength of rival great powers, used its existing colonies and newly acquired colonies in Africa and elsewhere, as easy export markets and as asylums for hundreds of thousands of its surplus population who were unable to find work at home.

7 JUBILEE YEARS

1881–1887

Jubilees in Britain have a disconcerting habit of arising at the most inappropriate times. The latest celebrations occurred when there were troubles in Ireland, massive unemployment at home, a high rate of inflation, and hard times for all but politicians and speculators. The silver jubilee of George V in 1935 was celebrated amid the worst sectarian riots in Belfast for many years, massive unemployment at home, moderate inflation, and hard times for all but politicians and speculators. Queen Victoria's jubilee in 1887, marking the first fifty years of her reign, occured at a time of troubles in Ireland, massive unemployment at home, deflation, and hard times for all but politicians and middlemen. Was it all coincidence, or is it that the English have been living out their own prolonged phantasy for the last century, in which only the details change, but no determined assaults are ever made on the persistent causes of the malady?

There were more fears, anxieties and violence in the years leading up to Queen Victoria's jubilee than there had been since the Hungry Forties. Earlier in the reign there had been very different attitudes towards the persistent problems of speculation, poverty and Ireland, a healthy self-confidence and an assurance that solutions might some day be found; but now there was a great sense of despair and despondency as it was realized that assaults on these hydra-headed problems only increased the vigour of their growth. There were widespread fears that the situation had got out of control; a new spirit of violence and anarchy was in the air.

The failure of Gladstone, or, indeed, of any other person, to solve the Irish question had already given it a nightmarish quality. Gladstone's first Land Act had done little to stop evictions and, as a consequence, Michael Davitt, a former Fenian, had founded the Irish Land League to fight evictions by new, and initially non-violent means. When peasants were evicted from their farms, other local residents refused to have any further dealings with either the agent or the new tenant. Captain Boycott, an English land agent in County Mayo, was one of the first victims of these new methods and his name was added to the English language to describe them. Almost inevitably, however, these boycotts often resulted in rick-burning, the killing of cattle and, sometimes, of tenants—by 'hired assassins', said Punch, or 'the Hidden Hand'.

Gladstone, who had become prime minister again in 1880, passed a new Land Act in the following year which gave the Irish peasants

much greater security of tenure and introduced a fair-rents system; but it came too late to halt the disorder. In the same year, Charles Stewart Parnell, the leader of the Irish MPs in the House of Commons and president of the Land League, was arrested and held without trial in Kilmainham gaol, Dublin, for allegedly inciting Land League members to violence. He was released in 1882 after making a pact with Gladstone. Parnell agreed to moderate the campaign while the prime minister promised to pass a Bill to wipe out rent arrears of Irish tenants. 'Ireland is to have a clean slate,' commented Punch sourly, 'and, as usual, at the expense of the British Taypayer. . . . The rent which the Irish malcontent can't, or won't, pay, and which the Irish landlord probably ought not to receive, is to be partly paid by the hard-working, over-taxed and much-abused Saxon.'

To reinforce his policy of conciliation, Gladstone sent Lord Frederick Cavendish as his new Chief Secretary to Ireland; but English public opinion was outraged when both he and Thomas Burke, the permanent under-secretary, were attacked by a gang of Irish extremists in Phoenix Park, Dublin, and savagely hacked to death with knives. Nine members of the Invincibles, as they called themselves, were arrested, and five of them were hanged; but violence continued unabated. On January 24, 1885, 'Ireland's worst enemies', Irish nationalists and American-Irish, planted bombs in three public buildings in London: one in the crypt leading out of Westminster Hall, another in the chamber of the House of Commons, and a third in the Tower of London. Five people were injured at Westminster, three of them seriously. These 'dynamite outrages' had been deliberately committed on a Saturday 'when the largest number of casual visitors was sure to be in the buildings destined to destruction, and when therefore the largest number of

Previous pages: Part of the procession in Parliament Square at Queen Victoria's Golden Jubilee celebrations in 1887

Opposite: Gladstone attacking 'the Irish devil-fish' (1881)

IRELAND'S WORST ENEMIES

On the part of London Irish Working Men, apprehension has been expressed that a prejudice against them, excited by the late Dynamite Outrages, supposed to have been committed by countrymen of theirs, will subject them to the loss or refusal of employment. As well think of disbanding the 'London Irish' Volunteers for fear of a Fenian 'Devil's Own'. It may surely be hoped that no employer of labour in England will so lose his head in a paroxysm of panic as to visit the atrocities of American-Irish miscreants on the heads of Anglo-Irish honest and good fellows. JOHN BULL is not the sort of Bull to go mad with fright, and behave with the unthinking fury of a frantic Bull in a China Shop. In the meanwhile, the Irish in our midst may well take note that the Dynamiters don't care a button what damage they may do them, whether by ruin of their means of living, or by blowing them up indiscriminately with their surrounding neighbours.

1885

innocent victims would be sent to their long rest without a note of warning, or, far worse, maimed, or blinded, or disfigured for life.'

By 1885, Gladstone had come to the conclusion that the only possible solution to the Irish problem was to grant the people of that troubled land, Home Rule. On April 8, 1886, he said in the House of Commons:

> We have sacrificed our time; we have neglected our own business; we have advanced our money—which I do not think at all a great favour conferred on her—and all this in an endeavour to give Ireland good laws. . . . But many of those laws have been passed under influences which can hardly be described otherwise than as influences of fear. Some of our laws have been passed in a spirit of grudging and jealousy. . . . Irish nationality vents itself in the demand for local autonomy, or separate and complete self-government in Irish, not in Imperial, affairs. Is this an evil in itself? Is it a thing that we should view with horror or apprehension?

Ninety-three members of his own party did, and, led by Joseph Chamberlain, voted against the first Home Rule Bill, and formed a Liberal Unionist group, which eventually amalgamated with the Conservatives. Gladstone introduced a second Home Rule Bill in 1893, but this was defeated in the House of Lords. The Irish problem refused to go away.

HARD TIMES

First City Man: When I began business I wasn't worth a penny.
Second City Man: Oh! And where are you now?
First City Man: Thousands in debt, sir! (1883)

Pater: Knowledge, my boy, is better than wealth——
Filius: Ye-es. But po'my word, d'you know, Sir, I think I prefer the inferior article! (1883)

Pater: Tom, Tom!—this'll never do. Past eleven o'clock!—and you've been in bed for fifteen hours out of the twenty-four!
Tom: But, it's cheap, Gov'nour—' costs nothing, Wh'r'as directly a fellow's up and dressed, expenses begin! (1887)

At home, as the Great Depression continued on its erratic course, there was deep gloom in the crisis years, relieved only by false hopes in others, when the economy seemed to be at last improving. In the hopeful years, Britain was already investing large sums overseas (an estimated £60 million for example in 1885), but owing to the global nature of the depression, both dividends and capital appreciation were sometimes minimal The Stock Exchange was more often down than up:

> I've tried my hand at Mexicans, and sold them in a funk
> And I've often been in and out of Canada's Grand Trunk;
> I've dabbled in Egyptians—you don't catch me there again—,
> I've lost in rails American—and burnt my hands in Spain.

British exporters increasingly found much of the advanced world blocked off by tariff barriers, but Britain still clung obstinately to its traditional policy of free trade long after many of its main competitors—the United States, Germany, France—had forsaken it. Other countries subsidized their exports. Germany and France, for example, gave subsidies for sugar exports so that British processors were unable to compete and were forced to close their plants. 'The philosophical free-trader', commented Punch in 1885, 'looks with calm indifference on the bitter sufferings of his own

'Unfair trade winds' (1884)

KURDS AND THEIR WAYS

It appears from an advertisement in the daily papers that the 'wild and terrible' Kurds, as they are called, in the intervals of their wildness and terror, are in the habit of making Persian carpets for the English market at very low prices. Perhaps if they were less wild and terrible, they would make worse carpets and charge higher prices. Civilisation is sometimes a great demoraliser.

1881

countrymen, rather than yield one tot, one tittle of the grand and noble principle that it is our duty as men, as brethren, and as Christians, to buy in the cheapest markets, be the consequences what they may.'

Britain had free trade, but was it also fair? Punch was convinced that it was not. 'Rings of middlemen, money-snatching monopolists' robbed 'producers and tradesmen of their legitimate

THE TELEGRAPH MONOPOLY

The Telegraph Monopoly—popularly known as the Post Office—is proving, if any proof were needed, that no Government can be trusted. Tory, Conservative, Liberal, or Radical, are all alike when the law gives them, or leads them to believe that it has given them, unlimited powers as traders. The so-called Post Office, having made a bad and improvident bargain with the Telegraph Companies, is determined to burke invention, and earn an evil reputation as the champion of everlasting stagnation. The impertinent inventors of the Telephone have been made aware of this in a court of law, and are now made even more bitterly aware of it in their subsequent negotiations with the Government.

In the first place they are told they must be taxed, and this is a communication they can hardly be astonished at. Nearly every living thing in this country is taxed, except vermin—the child in its cradle, the dying-man on his bed. The only thing practically exempt, is the corpse in its coffin. However sluggish the Government may be, the tax-gatherer is superhumanly active. A Government that once taxed the light of Heaven, can see no injustice in taxing a Telephone wire. In the second place, the impertinent inventors are told that their *radius* must be limited.

Because the Government wasted ten millions of public money in 1866, the Telephone Company may carry their wires to Stoke-Pogis and no further. The Cock-a-doodle-do policy in one department of Government, necessitated a money-grubbing policy in another. If this Government, that Government, or any other Government, had bought the Water Companies, half the kingdom would have been dying of thirst; and if they had bought the Stage-coach interest, railways would never have been built; or if built, would have been allowed no further than Hampstead and Camberwell.

1881

THE SCHOOL-BOARD VICTIM

'Mother! how my head is aching,
In a strange and painful way!
See what sad mistakes I'm making
In my exercise today.

'All the irksome words are whirling
Underneath my listless glance;
And the rows of figures curling
Round like demons in a dance.

'I was cold and wet and weary,
Hungry too, at school today.
Why is learning all so dreary?
Is there never time to play?'

So the School-Board victim crying,
Bowed her little aching head,
And her Mother watched her, sighing
For to-morrow's daily bread.

Oh, ye men of small discerning
On official red-tape nurst,
Though there's good no doubt in learning
We must feed the children first!

1883

profits, home manufacture of their credit, and the poor consumer of his chance of cheap commodities in secret, subtle, and sinister ways.' The medical journal, the *Lancet*, which had a great social conscience, revealed in 1885 that distributors of milk in the metropolis took 60 per cent of the price, leaving only the remaining 40 per cent for the producer. Middlemen also claimed their excessive pound of flesh in the meat and the fish trades. Punch quoted approvingly from the *British Trade Journal*:

> Between the starving farmers at one end of the line, and the starving workmen at the other, there is a row of jovial and rotund Middlemen, who, as cattle-dealers, drovers, salesmen, slaughterers, meat-carriers, and butchers, form a happy family unafflicted by the straits of the producer, and banded together at the expense of the purchasing Public.

There were similar malpractices in the manufacturing industries which furnished 'abundant chances for speculation and sharp practices, and for trading without sufficient capital or knowledge of business, to the detriment of the article, and the ruin of our reputation for commercial honesty.' British commission agents had but one aim, 'to pick up the largest possible profits'; but foreign competitors had a much more direct and intelligent system of distribution. Here was another problem which has refused to go away.

Economic mismanagement, speculation, and sweated labour combined to take a terrible toll among the submerged third of the

One of Punch's most famous cartoons and a perennial joke: 'I used your soap two years ago; since then I have used no other' (1884)

population living in desperate misery in metropolitan slums. Their abject poverty was already beginning to arouse a sense of shame. In 1881, under the title 'Great Britain?', Punch reported:

> The Government has published a parliamentary return in which it is obliged to admit that 101 persons died of absolute starvation in the Metropolitan district. This disgraceful record might be doubled or trebled if Coroners had the courage to call deaths by their right names.

England has always had its amiable eccentrics and in these desperate times, another Duke of Norfolk arose, this time in clerical guise, to suggest that if the poor could not afford to buy other foods, they might try eating insects instead. 'Stupidity to the Starving', growled Punch:

> They're excellent. The Reverend Sheppard
> Has tried Grasshoppers, freely peppered.
> The Grub of timber—plank or tub—
> Should be the toilers' daily 'grub',
> And neither beef nor veal is safer,
> At table, than the common Chafer.
> Wireworms, those eligible imps,
> Are a cheap substitute for shrimps . . .
> The very caterpillars cry
> 'Bake us with butter, boil and fry!'

Living conditions in the slums of London were atrocious with a dozen or more people often sharing the same small room with its bare boards, rotten rafters and vermin-eaten beds:

> Have you comfort for yourself and not for others?
> Are you careless of the future and its fate?
> In the name of great humanity, my brothers,
> Is it London that must wait?

'Slumming' became a fashionable pastime among the upper middle classes at that time, and play-groups for poor children were started in different parts of the capital, including one in 1885 in the parish of St Martin-in-the-Fields. To appease public opinion, the president of the Local Government Board visited the worst slums around the Angel in November 1883. A Royal Commission on the Housing of the Working Classes reported in 1885 on the slums of the metropolis and of other large cities, where, it said, the old houses were 'rotten from age and neglect' and the new houses were 'rotten from the first'. It made radical proposals for reform, including charging rates on empty building sites; cheap government loans to local authorities for slum clearance; and the demolition of London prisons to provide more sites for working-class homes. Although the Commission had many distinguished personages among its members, including the Prince of Wales, its recommendations were almost totally ignored.

It was almost inevitable that these exhortations should fail. A sense of unity can usually be summoned up in England only in the face of foreign enemies; in peace-time the nation remained as divided as it had been in Disraeli's *Sybil*, and as it still is to a

House-jobber: 'Now, then, my man; week's hup! Can't 'ave a 'ome without payin' for it, yer know!' (1883)

certain extent to this day, with each section of the community jealously guarding its own vested interests and making sure, when reforms were mooted, that it would not have to pay. City companies, aristocrats, and 'wealthy men, rich beyond the dreams of avarice', who owned 'nearly every foot of the freehold of the City', and much other property in London besides, were quite content to go on drawing their ground rents and watching the value of their sites increase year by year. Slum landlords were quite content to let their property rot, so long as they could secure a return of 50 per cent on their capital by letting squalid rooms at exorbitant rents to their doubly exploited tenants. The trade unions were quite content to exclude the worst-exploited workers from their organizations so long as they could continue to gain higher wages for their own skilled members. The middle classes were opposed in principle, and often in practice, to aristocrats, slum landlords and trade unions, but their beliefs did not extend to paying for the cost of change. When two London slums were demolished in 1883, Punch commented: 'The more rent these Vampires sucked out of the poor miserable tenants, the more

155

'THE BUSINESS OF THE NATION'

What *is* 'The business of the Nation'?
Endless row, roundaboutation,
Mutual spite and objurgation,
Egotistic self-inflation,
Partisan disintegration,
Venomous vilification,
Pettifogging aggravation,
General exasperation,
Universal degradation—
That's 'The business of the Nation',
As 'tis done in Parliament.
Is't not time the lot were sent,—
Ere BULL's brain is dazed to dizziness,—
Each and all, about *their* business?

1887

compensation they received from the City authorities, and the heavier Rates the City Rate-payers had to pay.' Other landlords put up their rents when new roads, paid for out of the rates, made their property more desirable. 'The only solution of this almost incredible state of law is, that the Legislature consists almost entirely of Landlords, who apparently rejoice in devising laws whose evident effect must be to make the idle and the rich owner much richer, and the hard-working and comparatively poor

BANKRUPTCY FOR THE MILLION

There was a time when the rich had a monopoly of all the luxuries, and the poor had to be content with the leavings of the rich. Many years of free-trade, liberal government, and penny newspapers have changed the order of things, and now the most venerated delicacies are brought within the reach of the multitude. Early strawberries, plovers' eggs, asparagus, ortolans, and green peas are as plentiful as blackberries—more plentiful we are glad to say, as we never relished blackberries; and even bankruptcy, which was once the exclusive luxury of the aristocratic trader, is now to be as common as excursion trains or fourteen shilling trousers.
Mr. CHAMBERLAIN has brought in a Bill which proposes to give a creditor for the paltry sum of £20 the power to issue a fiat, and which also proposes to abolish the special protection accorded to Members of Parliament. A debtor who cannot or will not pay his tailor's bill is now to be treated with as much consideration as a 'merchant prince', and unpaid milk-scores are to rub shoulders with the greatest financial swindles. The blue-blood of insolvency ought to rise against such insolvent Radicalism, before the Church, the House of Lords, the LORD CHAMBERLAIN, and the Meddlevex Magistrates are swallowed up in the general vortex.

1881

occupier much poorer.' The logic of these views might have led to socialism, as it did for a handful of the middle classes who had just banded together as Fabians; but the vast majority of the middle classes were even more opposed to socialists than they were to landlords and Punch concluded conservatively that the real remedy for this 'gross injustice' was the formation of ratepayers' associations.

Some of the workers were more willing to follow the logic of such arguments. The red flag flew at meetings and in the streets and brigades of the unemployed drilled in secret. The president of the English National Revolutionary League declared in language which was very similar to that used by Punch in its radical origins, that kings and priests should be swept away as 'emblems of tyranny and force and fraud' but such revolutionary sentiments no longer roused any sympathetic vibrations in Punch, only fear and derision:

> Altar and throne shall come down,
> Smashed by the red revolution,
> All institutions are bosh,
> Mankind, we know, doesn't need 'em;
> Here's to the men, who don't wash,
> Dirt is the emblem of Freedom!

In 1886, when unemployment, in one of its periodic upsurges, had reached an estimated 10 per cent, a procession of the workless ran amuck in Pall Mall, shattering the windows of gentlemen's clubs. Both radicals and conservatives believed that the revolution was very near. Punch was as shocked by the inactivity of Colonel Henderson, the Commissioner of the Metropolitan Police, as it was by the 'maddened Mob' and designed a fanciful uniform for the riot police who would be much needed in the future.

The growth of violence at home was matched by an increasing number of wars overseas. In 1881 the 'boring' Boers started to give trouble again. Although they had been quite prepared to relinquish their independence so that Britain would protect them from the Zulus, they wanted their freedom back again now that the danger was past. In a brief war they gained a quick victory over the British in the battle of Majuba Hill, Natal, mainly through their skills in marksmanship and sniping which they were to use with even more deadly effect in the second Boer War at the end of the reign. Punch was disgusted:

> BRITANNIA needs instruction
> To teach her boys to shoot,
> Fixed targets and mere red-tape drill
> Have borne but bitter fruit.

Gladstone, who was no imperialist, was glad to restore independence to the Boers of the Transvaal. But with Britain's need for new markets, raw materials and mineral wealth, Gladstone was inexorably propelled to follow in Dizzy's footsteps, whether he wished to do so or not, by expanding overseas territories, where

Anarchy and socialism struck fear into the middle classes in the 1880s

Above left: *Spirit of Anarchy:* 'What! No work! Come and enlist with me,—I'll find work for you!!' (1886)

Above right: 'Sowing tares (with a thousand apologies to Sir John E. Millais, Bart, R.A.)' (1886)

Britain already had a foothold, or by acquiring new colonies where it had none. In 1882, Britain took over Egypt as a protectorate after a quick campaign in which the British army proved that it was more of a match for Egyptian natives than for white Boers. 'A short innings, but a good one,' commented Punch complacently, for once. Three years later, Bechuanaland, in southern Africa, also became a protectorate; while in the Far East, British troops from their bases in Rangoon launched an attack on the Burmese to take over the rest of their country.

The involvement in Egypt led to one of those death-or-glory sagas which have always stirred the imagination of the English people. The Sudan, which was then ruled by Egypt, was ablaze with a revolt led by Mohammed Ahmed, who had assumed the title of Mahdi, or Messiah. In 1884 the British government appointed General Gordon to evacuate the isolated garrisons of Egyptian troops from the Sudan; but Gordon, or 'Chinese Gordon'

MTESA

UGANDA's king is dead! The great black city
No more shall know its lord. *M'tesa* pity!

1885

THE RANGE OF POSSIBILITY

1871 Major WATKINS invents a range-finder of the greatest possible utility.
1872 War Office Officials consider experiments satisfactory.
1873 Somebody reports upon it.
1874 Someone else 'hangs it up'.
1875 No time this year to proceed with it.
1876 Someone forgets all about it.
1877 Nothing done. Stagnation.
1878 Inventor revives it.
1879 Inventor snubbed.
1880 More experiments and more successes.
1881 Invention again pigeon-holed.
1882 Still 'under consideration'.
1883 Invention declared perfection.
1884 Government uncertain.
1885 Matter further shelved.
1886 Somebody takes an interest in it.
1887 DUKE of CAMBRIDGE looks at it.
1888 Invention purchased!

1888

Relief forces failed to save General Gordon in Khartoum as Britannia cries 'Too late!' (1885)

as he was popularly known through his many victories in the Far East, was no more intimidated by a black skin than he was by a yellow one. But he had under-estimated the strength of the Mahdi and his dervishes and soon found himself isolated and cut off in Khartoum. After numerous hesitations, Gladstone reluctantly decided to send out a relief force from England to rescue Gordon, but he was killed two days before it reached Khartoum. From afar, the British public read reports, with mingled feelings of fascination and horror, of the long slow march south to rescue one of their most popular generals, who had been besieged for ten months. When it was learnt that relief had arrived too late, Gladstone was villified for his hesitations and inefficiency; but, as with the Charge of the Light Brigade, the incompetence was forgotten more quickly than the glory, and Gordon became part of imperialist folklore:

> Firm, whilst a hundred perils round thee thicken
> Hourly, and hourly fades the hope of aid
> From England. Through the Desert night's dusk shade
> We watch thee send that vigilant gaze in vain
> Across the silent sand-flats mile on mile;
> To death resigned, unwitting that the while
> Thy brave belated brethren toil and strain
> Towards thee o'er the Nile.

Neither Gordon's heroic stand nor anticipation of the jubilee could really extirpate the mood of gloom and depression, which flattened even Mr Punch's usually effervescent feelings in these long-drawn-out years. The editor, Tom Taylor, had died in 1880 and

was succeeded by F C Burnand, but this change of control was not responsible for the dejection, as Burnand was more lively and extraverted than his scholarly predecessor. No, Punch, in those years was faithfully reflecting the general mood of oppression, uncertainty and fear, feelings which are manifested in many other source materials of the time. We have only to compare the jubilation and excitement that greeted the Great Exhibition of 1851 with the rather dulled sense of celebration at the jubilee to see that there had been a very marked change in attitudes.

Many different organizations used the opportunity, as they always do, to exact some financial tribute from the public. The Prince of Wales appealed for money for the Imperial Institute; the Crystal Palace, which was becoming something of a white elephant, tried to raise more funds; and the Hospital for Sick Children in Great Ormond Street launched a more modest appeal for £16,000. London's solicitors entertained a thousand of their country cousins to a banquet in the central hall of the Royal Courts of Justice; Henry Irving gave children a jubilee performance of *Werner* with Ellen Terry in the part of Josephine; while the Queen went off to West Kensington for a private Royal Command performance of Colonel Cody's Wild West show.

The jubilee on June 21, 1887 was an even bigger show. Thousands of people lined the route to watch the procession to Westminster Abbey, which included sixteen princes on horseback and many foreign potentates. The Marquis of Lorne distinguished himself by falling off his horse, but he was soon remounted on another. Mr Punch was critical, as well he might be, of the many people who threw coins on to the procession from high windows; of the closed carriages which prevented spectators from getting a clear view of the occupants; and of the three bands in Trafalgar Square which played music of the dullest sort. His spirits revived a little at the celebrations later in the day at the Crystal Palace, which included an open-air ballet performance and a fireworks display. But the really touching part of the whole celebrations for him occurred during the impressive ceremony in the Abbey when the Queen 'turned round to receive the homage of her children, and insisted, contrary to all precedent, upon kissing them.' It was

Punch's prophetic view of 'The police of the future' (1886)

A DAINTY DISH TO SET BEFORE THE QUEEN

Let all merry children subscribe to complete
The House for Sick Children in Great Ormond Street!
They want Sixteen Thousand to make it all right—
A pretty round sum—let each mite give its mite;
The Children of England will raise, you'll soon see,
A Fund to thus honour the QUEEN'S Jubilee.

1887

during those moments that 'the People realised once again how intensely womanly their Sovereign Lady was, and why they not only respected and admired, but loved her.'

When the great day was over, the British lion, rather limp from exertion and hoarse from roaring, decided that it was time to get back to business again. Events would not wait. Only a few months later the unemployed tried to storm Trafalgar Square and one of the demonstrators died from injuries he received in clashes with the police. The first jubilee of Queen Victoria gave the English people only a fleeting glimpse of the sun through the dark clouds; they would have to wait another ten years for a different dawn.

OUR BILL FOR LONDON IMPROVEMENTS

Have we not weather in London nearly equal to that of Paris? Haven't we nearly as many days of heat without rain during the Summer? We advisedly qualify our question with 'nearly' because we are only about to suggest what can be done with 'nearly' as many open-air refreshment-places.

1. Restaurants in the gardens on the Thames Embankment. Lower the iron-railings, so as to give a good view of the Thames, and let there be central entrances, in addition to those now existing. These Restaurants to be open till 12.30. Virginia and other fast growing creepers to be trained all over the structures belonging to the District Railway.

2. The entire length of the Embankment to be lighted by electricity.

3. In future, wherever a new Restaurant is to be built in Regent Street, Oxford Street, Shaftesbury Avenue, and so forth, the frontage shall not abut the pavement, but be so far back as to leave plenty of space for taking refreshment out-of-doors.

4. That trees be at once planted all along Regent Street, Portland Place, and Oxford Street, and their number be increased in the new Avenues.

5. That there be a good Restaurant in Kensington Gardens, with abundance of small tables and chairs, and ample attendance. Private rooms for dinners etc., and a terrace under cover for meals *al fresco* at all times of the day. Open on Sundays. Band to play at certain hours.

6. Another Restaurant on a similar scale, to be in Hyde Park, in central situation. Both these to be lighted by electric light. . . .

1889

Henry Irving put on a special performance for children in celebration of the Jubilee (1887)

8 EXPANDING HORIZONS

1888–1896

Although his health and vigour had not been entirely restored, John Bull was encouraged to find that each of the worst bouts of depression—in 1876, 1886 and 1893—appeared to be somewhat less virulent than the last. He was learning to live with his condition. Even though he might never be able to regain his former sense of well-being, it was better to laugh at his troubles, until some government of the future deprived him of that final freedom. It was obvious that strikes and violence were going to be part of the established disorder of the future, as they were no longer confined only to skilled workers, or even to men. Much to his amazement, seven hundred women workers stopped work in a London match factory in 1888 and marched out to demand better pay and conditions. In the following year, the dockers went on strike for a minimum wage of sixpence an hour, and for the first time for nearly a century, the London docks, the heart of imperial trade, were still and silent. And, of course, those champagne-quaffing miners still stopped work with the regularity of unthinking automatons:

NOT NEGOTIABLE

Impecunious Lodger: Jemima, did you ask Mrs. Maggles whether she would take my I.O.U. for this quarter's rent, as I'm rather——
Maid of all work: Yes, sir, and she say she won't sir, not if you was to hoffer 'er the 'ole halphabit! (1889)

WAYS AND MEANS

Visitor: You take it easy, Brown. You must have a good salary.
Brown: H-m—Ya-as—pre'y well. I draw three hundred a year—save say a hundred, and run into debt four hundred, that's—eight hundred; and if a bachelor can't live on that—'ought to be ashamed of himself! (1888)

TRAM-CAR TRAMMELS

We are told that London Tram-car men are kept on their feet some sixteen hours at a stretch. Poor fellows! *Mr. Punch* wonders they stand it, and feels that they—and a sympathetic Public—ought to make a stand against it! Let Public Opinion, as imperatively as the old highwayman, bid the Monopolists 'Stand and deliver' these poor tram-slaves from their tedious thraldom!

1889

Mechanic: Hullo, Jem! Not at work? What's up?
Collier: Oh, we're out on strike.
Mechanic: What for then?
Collier: Aw diven knaw, but we'll not give in till we get it!

Socialism was also gaining new adherents among the working classes and within three years of the London dock strike it had succeeded in battering down the privileged portals of the House of Commons. Although there had been a handful of working-class MPs since 1874—the original Lib-Labs—they had all sat on the Liberal benches; but in 1892, three independent Labour members were elected, including the bearded John Burns, who had led the London dock strike, and Keir Hardie, who was said to have entered the House wearing a working-man's cloth cap, a story he later denied.

While socialists and strikers were chalking up their victories, the new women continued on their long, slow march towards emancipation and equality. They had replaced male linen-draper assistants behind many a counter after a long campaign which had begun before the Crimean War; they served customers—or chatted with each other, said Punch—in post offices; and some women even cut men's hair. The invention of the typewriter in the 1870s had provided a new occupation for them as typists, or lady-typewriters, as they were first called, a career which was a virtual female monopoly from the start. More women students were going to Oxford and to Cambridge, though none of them was granted the privilege of receiving a degree until after the First World War; but London University was less unbending and gave degrees to women from 1878. The first appearance of lady graduates in Convocation in 1884 received a rather ambiguous welcome in Punch:

> Thus Woman wins. Haul down your flag
> Oh, stern misogynist, before her.
> However much a man may brag
> Of independence, he'll adore her.

New women were no longer willing to accept their former strait-laced existence, symbolized by the corset which painfully gripped their waists within an eighteen-inch whale-bone vice; aesthetic women had thrown away their corsets in the 1880s and wore a much looser and flowing costume, which by the following decade

Previous pages: Bicycling in a London park in about 1895

Above: Leg-of-mutton sleeves, were the latest fashion in the Nineties. The precocious child asks: 'Oh, mummy, have you been vaccinated on *both* arms?' (1893)

THE NEW WOMEN

They dress . . . like men.
They talk . . . like men.
They live . . . like men.
They don't . . . like men.

1895

Above left: 'Counter-irritation. A study at a winter sale' (1895)

Above right: Punch mocked any kind of woman who took up activities previously reserved for men. *The vicar's wife:* 'And have you had good sport Miss Goldenberg?' *Miss Goldenberg:* 'Oh, rippin! I only shot one rabbit, but I managed to injure quite a dozen more' (1894)

had become more severe and somewhat masculine with stand-up collars and wide striped ties. More young girls smoked cigarettes openly at home, and demanded that, like their brothers, they should have their own *Wanderjahr*, in which they might travel or live alone in lodgings while they studied, and experienced life. They wanted to come and go as they pleased: the latch-key question caused many rifts between new women and their mammas in the 1890s. 'I never allowed my husband to have one till he was

---

AESTHETIC LOVE IN A COTTAGE

Miss Bilderbogie: Yes, dearest Joconda! I am going to marry young Peter Pilcox! We shall be very, *very* poor! Indeed how we are going to *live*, I cannot tell!
Mrs. Cimabue Brown: Oh, my beautiful Mariana, how *noble* of you both! Never mind *how*, but *where* are you going to live?
Miss Bilderbogie: Oh, in dear old Kensington, I suppose— everything is so cheap there, you know!—peacock feathers only a *penny a-piece!*

1881

---

forty-nine', wrote one indignant *Mother of Three* in Punch. 'I sometimes regret I ever gave one to him, though as it is we always chain the door at eleven o'clock.'

Although new women found it difficult to emancipate themselves from the bonds of masculine prejudice, particularly where property, wealth, employment and government were involved, they were able to win great victories on the playing fields of England. By the 1890s women were playing golf; cricket, in which W G Grace had scored a century of centuries by 1895; and, much to Mr Punch's disgust, even climbing in the Alps in most unfeminine costumes:

> You who look, at home, so charming—
> Angel, goddess, nothing less—
> Do you know you're quite alarming
>   In that dress?
> Such a garb should be forbidden;
> Where's the grace an artist loves?
> Think of dainty fingers hidden
>   In those gloves?

Above: The alpine climber (1893)

Opposite: Sport played a great part in the emancipation of women (1891)

THE RULES OF THE RUDE

1. The one object which all cyclists should keep steadily in view is to become 'scorchers'. There are three essentials before you can earn this proud title. First, you must totally disregard the convenience or safety of the public. Second, you must ride at a minimum rate of 15 miles an hour. Third, you must develop pronounced curvature of the spine as quickly as is compatible with your other engagements.

2. Races should always be held on the high roads, at a time of the day when traffic is busiest.

3. Should you be unfortunate enough to knock down a pedestrian, do not trouble to stop and apologise, or inquire if he's hurt. It is his business to get out of your way, and you should remind him of this obligation in the most forcible language at your disposal. This will tend to make the pastime exceedingly popular among non-cyclists.

4. If you notice an old gentleman crossing the road, wait till you get quite close to him, them emit a wild war-whoop, blow your trumpet, and enjoy the roaring fun of seeing what a shock you have given him.

5. A still better plan, if a wayfarer happens to be walking in the middle of the road, and going in your own direction, is *not* to signal your approach at all, but to startle him into fits by suddenly and silently gliding by him when he believes himself to be quite alone. The nearer you can shave his person the better the sport.

6. Of course the last plan is much improved if the wayfarer should be a market woman carrying milk or eggs, and if in her fright she drops her can or basket. Unfortunately few cyclists have the good fortune to witness this exquisite bit of rural comedy.

These Rules will now probably be thoroughly revised, as the 'National Cyclists' Union' has issued a well-timed manifesto warning all wheelmen against 'furious riding'.)

1893

PAST AND PRESENT.

IN THE SIXTIES.

IN THE SEVENTIES.

IN THE EIGHTIES.

IN THE NINETIES.

Half a century before, Mrs Amelia Bloomer had campaigned unsuccessfully for more rational clothes for women, but it was the bicycle which eventually persuaded thousands of ordinary women to wear the very kind of garment that her arguments had failed to make them adopt. The velocipede and the penny-farthing had been manias for the few, but men and women of all classes took up cycling when the modern safety bicycle started to be produced on a large scale in the 1890s. (The first practical machine, with a chain-driven rear wheel, was made by J K Starley of Coventry in 1885 and J B Dunlop added pneumatic tyres three years later.) Even the Prince of Wales—now the 'Prince of Wheels' for Mr Punch—started cycling in 1896 at the age of fifty-five. Although there was a lady's version of the bicycle, without a cross-bar and with a chain guard, many women found conventional clothes unsuitable for cycling and preferred to wear a bifurcated skirt or bloomers, which, ironically, were 'vindicated in Dame Fashion's eyes' in the very year of their promoter's death in 1894. With so many women adopting masculine attire 'angry old buffers' began to wonder just what the world was coming to:

> Tomorrow there may be *no* sexes!
> Unless, as end to all the pother,
> Each one in fact becomes the other.

'Things are not always what they seem. Below is not a cowardly attack upon an unprotected lady cyclist, but merely Tom giving his heart's idol her first lesson' (1896)

SUBACIDITIES

Gladys: Oh, Muriel dear, that heavenly frock! I think it looks lovelier every year!! (1893)

—There go the Spicer Wilcoxes, Mamma! I'm told they're dying to know us. Hadn't we better call?
—Certainly not, dear. If they're dying to know us, they're not worth knowing. The only people worth *our* knowing are the people who *don't* want to know us. (1892)

Angelina: Incomes under £150 a year are exempt from income-tax. Isn't it lucky, darling? We just miss it by five pounds. (1890)

She: How silent you are! What are you thinking of?
He: Nothing!
She: Egotist! (1890)

Cousin Jack: Then why did you marry him, Effie?
Effie: Oh well, I wanted to see the Paris Exhibition, you know! (1890)

Mrs. Wistful: What happy people you are to have six nice daughters. What resources for your old age.

Mr. Quiverful: Yes. Resources enough! But the difficulty nowadays, consists in *husbanding* one's resources. (1888)

There was an even newer kind of woman abroad, indistinguishable in appearance, according to Mr Punch, from any conventional English beauty in their long flowing gowns with square-cut necks and leg-of-mutton sleeves, which were sometimes so huge that they had to be artificially padded out with cushions; but with very different attitudes, which were far more direct and less pretentious. These American women, like their younger brothers, had no respect for the social conventions of the decadent and divided Europe from which their fathers or their ancestors had fled.

A young American boy interrupts the conversation between his mother and an English bishop on a transatlantic steamer:

The Bishop (severely): When *I* was your age, my young friend, it was not considered good manners for little boys to join in the conversation of grown-up people, unless they were invited to do so.

Small American: Guess that was seventy or eighty years ago. We've changed all that, you bet!

In her own inimitable and aphoristic way, one pert young American miss epitomized the main theory of that great American sociologist, Thorstein Veblen, five years before he had published his classic work, *The Theory of the Leisure Class*:

He: The worst of you Americans is that you have no leisure class.

She: Yes, we have. We call them *tramps*!

These wealthy heiresses, descendants from their surnames of the original Dutch settlers on Manhattan Island, or daughters of the *nouveaux riche* owners of mid-west shambles, the 'Chicago belles', may have been rather rough diamonds, but they were glittering prizes for the polished, but hard-pressed, English aristocrats of the times. Unlike some of the continental nobility, who have preserved the exclusive pride of their self-contained caste at the cost of poverty, English aristocrats, even of great rank and lineage, have long had a sharp eye for the main commercial chance. Some of them had been forced to reduce, or even to remit, farm rents on their vast estates during the continuing agricultural depression, and the revival of their fortunes was further delayed by the refusal of many conservative English farmers to change to more profitable forms of production. The introduction of death duties by the Liberals in 1894 was another heavy blow for the depressed dukes:

> *Duke of Devonshire:* If this Budget passes, I don't know *how* I'm going to keep up Chatsworth!
> *Duke of Westminster:* If you come to that, we may consider ourselves lucky if we can keep a tomb over our heads!

Punch, which had never had much sympathy with the plight of aristocrats, was delighted to mock their new distress. Two fashionable ladies of the upper middle classes meet in the park:

> By the by, I wish you could get me a card for the Duchess of Beaumorris's dance.
> I'll try. But you'll have to get a costume from her, or a bonnet, or *something*—as she only asks her *customers*!

Many aristocrats chose to take a less arduous way out of their temporary financial difficulties: Punch observed that 'the more respectable among English dukes, and the bluer blood of English gentlemen, are finding brides in the United States'. The most historic match occurred in 1874 when Lord Randolph Churchill, the third son of the Duke of Marlborough, married Jennie Jerome of New York, their first son, Winston, being born in the same year. English aristocrats hawked their coronets across the Atlantic; rich American men travelled the other way in search of a title. The

---

THINGS ONE WOULD HAVE WISHED TO EXPRESS DIFFERENTLY

Nervous invalid: Ah, my dear fellow, this is one of the worst attacks I ever had!
Sympathetic Friend: Yes, old man—I sincerely hope *it will be the last*! Goodbye! (1889)

—You can't go home when it's raining like this. You'd better stay and have dinner with us.
—Oh, it's not quite so bad as *that*! (1889)

Musical Maiden: I hope I am not boring you, playing so much?
Enamoured Youth: Oh no! Pray go on! I-I'd so much sooner hear you play than talk! (1882)

TIPS FOR FARMERS

Stick to wheat. It was good enough for your forefathers, and ought to be good enough for you.

Clamour for protection. There is not the slightest chance of your getting it, but it can do no harm to ask for it, and it takes your mind off such comparatively unimportant subjects as rent, compensation for improvement, and so on.

Leave your soil alone. Don't spend money on nitrates or other new-fangled devices for increasing its fertility. If it grows weeds, as it probably does, it can grow other things if it likes. Don't humour it.

Never plant a fruit tree. Fruit encourages birds (and boys) to steal. If anybody suggests jam, tell him 'you are not a grocer' and see what he says. The probability is, that he can say nothing in face of such a smashing retort.

Never co-operate with neighbouring farmers, in spite of what Lord WINCHILSEA urges. That sort of thing may suit the poor despised Dane, but not the free Briton. As a rule, the worse terms you are on with brother-farmers, the better.

Eggs are entirely beneath your dignity. So are poultry. So are most other things. You might do a little stock-raising, but only in a casual way. Cows are a nuisance; let nothing tempt you into the absurd 'fad' of dairy-farming. It's the sort of thing for milkmaids and milksops, not for you.

Keep no accounts. Never read anything about your business. If the world moves, decline to move with it. You will find this course the simplest, and the Official Receiver a very pleasant gentleman, after all.

1896

John Bull bids farewell his new ally Uncle Sam, in the uniform of the Honourable Artillery Company of Boston (1896)

multi-millionaire, William Waldorf Astor, settled permanently in England and eventually became a citizen and the first viscount. In 1893 he bought both the *Pall Mall Gazette* and Cliveden. Punch accepted these reversals of fortune with remarkable fortitude and prescience:

> When the Dollar dictates shall mere patriots kick?
> Our hills and our forests? If oil-kings appear
> And want them—for cash—as preserves for their deer,
> Down, down with mere pride.

Despite economic and colonial rivalries, relations with the United States and Germany were closer than they had been for some years, though both friendships were to be temporarily soured before the Diamond Jubilee by disputes in South America and South Africa respectively. In 1891, the Kaiser, Wilhelm II (who, in Punch's immortal words, had just dropped the pilot, Bismarck), paid a visit to his grandmother, Queen Victoria, and received a much more rapturous reception from the nation than he had done three years before. The Ancient and Honourable Artillery Company of Boston, whose members were mainly east-coast aristocrats, including some descendants of the original Pilgrim

171

Fathers, visited the Honourable Artillery Company of London and were also received by the Queen at Windsor. These visits helped to sustain the mystical spirit of white supremacy, which arose in this age of new imperialism, when many European nations—England, France, Germany, Belgium and Portugal—became involved in the scramble for Africa, and when even the anti-imperialist United States took over Cuba, the Philippines and Puerto Rico after the Spanish-American War of 1898. Imperialism was encouraged in England by the belief of Cecil Rhodes in the divine right of the English-speaking people to rule, and by Joseph Chamberlain's support as colonial secretary for imperial federation and, later, an alliance with Germany.

As the biggest imperial power, England took the lion's share in Africa. The Gold Coast, now part of Ghana, was acquired in 1874. Nigeria became a protectorate in 1885 and a colony five years later. In 1888 an Imperial British East Africa Company was granted a Royal Charter and within a few years it had taken over Zanzibar, Uganda and Kenya. In 1898, Kitchener finally avenged the death of Gordon by his slaughter of the dervishes at the battle of Omdurman, and the Sudan came under the joint rule of Britain and Egypt.

But it was southern Africa, with its vast unexploited stores of minerals which dazzled European eyes with its hopes of unparalleled wealth, such as Cecil Rhodes had exploited in the diamond mines of Kimberley and later in the Rand, where the biggest goldfield in the world had been discovered in 1886. Rhodes had gone out to South Africa for health reasons as a seventeen-year-old lad in 1870 and had soon become a multi-millionaire. He decided to use his vast fortune to build up a great new British empire in Africa. In 1889, his British South African Company was granted a Royal Charter and shortly afterwards a small force of two hundred employees accompanied by five hundred Company policemen set out on their long march to the north. By the following year they had established a settlement at Salisbury, which became the capital of the country which was named after their employer. In 1895, Rhodes attempted to increase his power in southern Africa by sending an employee, Dr L Starr Jameson, with a band of nearly five hundred horsemen into the Transvaal to provoke an uprising against the Boer government among the British workers in the Rand goldfields, the *Uitlanders*. The Jameson raid was a complete failure and Rhodes was forced to resign from the premiership of Cape Colony.

Punch was still not entirely bemused by dreams of imperial glory, believing that 'The March of Civilisation' would lead only to devastating wars among the newly-armed colonial nations. It had no admiration either for Rudyard Kipling, possibly through professional jealousy of his success in depicting the thoughts and feelings of common soldiers, which the magazine thought of as its own monopoly. Kipling's *Barrack Room Ballads* were scathingly

'Good-bye, grandmamma.' The Kaiser, Wilhelm II bids farewell to Queen Victoria after his successful visit to Britain which helped to improve relations, temporarily, between the two countries (1891)

UNEMPLOYED HEROES

A Discharged Soldier's Aid Society is doing what it can to supply a considerable oversight on the part of a grateful, rather than thoughtful country. It is hardly meet that poor TOMMY ATKINS, who has spent the best years of his life in his country's service, should be turned adrift to take the consequence of his unavoidable improvidence amongst the 'unemployed'. There is also a Society for the Aid of Discharged Prisoners; but the aid afforded to TOMMY should be proportioned to his deserts, which somewhat exceed those of JEMMY—so to denominate a burglar—can reasonably expect to receive.

Mr. Punch wishes success to the D.S.A.S., for it is hard on TOMMY to treat him as a boy treats an orange, which, after he has sucked it dry, he chucks into the gutter.

1888

THE MARCH OF CIVILISATION

(From a Record in the Far East)

Step One.—The nation takes to learning the English language.
Step Two.—Having learned the English language, the nation begins to read British newspapers.
Step Three.—Having mastered the meaning of the leaders, the nation start a Parliament.
Step Four.—Having got a Parliament, the nation establishes school boards, railways, stockbrokers, and penny ices.
Step Five.—Having become fairly civilised, the nation takes up art and commerce.
Step Six.—Having realised considerable wealth, the nation purchases any amount of ironclads, heavy ordnance, and ammunition.
Step Seven.—Having the means within reach, the nation indulges in a terrific war.
Step Eight.—Having lost everything, the nation returns with a sigh of relief to old-fashioned barbarism.

1894

'Wooing the African Venus.' Punch, now imperialist, celebrates the granting of a charter to the British East Africa Company to develop thousands of square miles of fertile land (1888)

dismissed as 'a jumble of words without a trace of swing or music. All this Tommy Atkins business, with its "Rookies" and its "Johnny Raws", and its affectation of intimate knowledge of the common soldier's inmost feelings, is about played out. . . .'

Rhodes was different. His vision of a great British empire, linked by telegraph, stretching from the Cape to Cairo, combined 'in one supernatural blend' both commerce and the imagination. The dreams of this 'seven-league-booted Colossus', who had a striking facial resemblance to Hitler, expanded the horizons of a nation which was still not quite sure whether it had found its true path again:

Hooray! We brave Britons are still to the front—
Provided we've someone to boss us—to boss us;
And Scuttlers will have their work cut out to shunt
This stalwart, far-striding Colossus—Colossus!

As Disraeli had foreseen, imperialism was the only path which could lead back quickly to greatness again.

At home, the middle classes were beginning to congeal into a more solidified caste with its own conceits and culture, as dividends became more important than enterprise, and security became more attractive than risk. Burnand greatly expanded the coverage of the arts and of literature in the facetiously named *Booking Office*. Baiting the aesthetes, the intellectuals and the *avant-garde* helped to reaffirm the philistine values of the middle classes in a world which was rapidly changing in so many different ways, intellectually, socially, politically, technologically. The favourite targets for abuse were Oscar Wilde; Aubrey Beardsley; Thomas Hardy, 'Dude the Diffuse' by 'Toomuch Too Hardy'; and Ibsen. *Hedda Gabler*, was 'poor stuff and pernicious nonsense' which 'would scarcely have been allowed a second night's

---

A LONDON PEST

To an impartial observer the public, philanthropic, and municipal attempts to honour the memory of the great and good, if sometimes mistaken, Earl of SHAFTESBURY, appear to have been singularly unfortunate. The West-End Avenue that bears his name is more full of music-halls, theatres, pot houses, and curious property, than any street of equal length and breadth in the whole Metropolis. Lord SHAFTESBURY may not have been a Puritan, but he was essentially a serious man, and his sympathies were more with Exeter Hall than with the Argyll Rooms; and yet, in the street which is honoured by his name, it has been found impossible to remove the old title of this historic place from the stone *façade* of the Trocadero.

The fountain at Piccadilly Circus, which has been unveiled as the second of the SHAFTESBURY memorials, is surmounted by—what? Some writers have called it a girl, some have called it a boy; many of the public, no doubt, regard it as a mythological bird, and it certainly looks like the Bolognese Mercury flying away with the wings of St. Michael. We are told, on authority, that it represents Eros, the Greek god of love, and his shaft is directed to a part of London that, more than any other part, at night, requires the bull's-eye and the besom of authority. The 'Top of the Gaymarket' is in just as bad a condition as it was when *Punch* directed attention to it more than ten years ago, and the virus since then has extended as far eastwards as St. Martin's Lane. Moll Flanders Parade now begins at St. James's Church and ends with Cranbourne Street. It is unfortunate, to say the least of it, that Eros has been selected to point at this London Pestiduct, and the sooner it is thoroughly cleansed and the neighbourhood made worthy of the Shaftesbury Fountain, the better.

1893

---

existence at the Vaudeville'. Many of the middle classes were only too glad to close their minds to all that was new, and mentally or emotionally disturbing, in the cause of greater security and consolidation. Expansion overseas contracted vigour at home.

Floral hats were all the vogue in the Nineties. The original caption read: *Hyde Park loafer:* 'Want a gard'ner, Miss?' (1896)

9 SIXTY GLORIOUS YEARS

1897–1901

Circumstances seemed far more propitious for the Diamond Jubilee than they had been for the fifty-year commemoration only a decade before, even though there were still doubts and uncertainties, and potentially alarming portents for the economic future as employers and workers in major industries, such as mining and shipbuilding, froze into static postures of defiance and antagonism which were to be maintained for many generations. Already, in the jubilee year itself, one of the periodic strikes and lock-outs in the shipbuilding industry had robbed British yards of a valuable contract for an armoured cruiser, which the Japanese government had then transferred to France. Punch had little patience with either employers or unions.

> Ye demagogues of England,
> That draw your Union's fees,
> And smile to watch our foreign trade
> Drift out across the seas! . . .
>
> Capitalists of England!
> How long shall these things be?
> How long shall labour idly stand
> Barred out with lock and key?

And a mere couple of years away, had the Victorians only known, lay the even greater international humiliation of the Boer War—England's own Vietnam—when forty thousand guerrillas were to mock the might of half a million troops of the greatest imperial power in the world, fighting alone and unsupported by most of the major powers in the eroded scrubland of the South African veld.

Fortunately, however, that abasement was still veiled by the future. Furthermore, the diamond jubilee was an occasion not for anticipating what was to be, but far more for reflecting on what had been achieved during sixty glorious years, and particularly in the last decade. The ambitions of the queen, who was now seventy-eight years of age, may have been very different in those distant days, beyond the recall of many English men and women, when she had ascended the throne as a young girl on the death of her uncle, William IV in 1837; but, in spite of all the chaotic shifts of fortune in the following sixty years, she had succeeded in maintaining the greatness of Britain, and even added to it. In the ten years between the two jubilees, Britain had increased the size of its overseas territories by some five million square miles—fifty times the area of the mother country—making it the greatest power the world

179

had ever known with an empire on which the sun never literally set. In origin it may have been Dizzy's dream more than hers, but she had supported and encouraged it. The homage of the nation, and of the Empire, was her rightful due.

There was a burgeoning excitement, very different from the withered growth which had preceded the previous jubilee, as 'the Queen's Year' approached; and heartfelt relief as the crucial date of September 23, 1896 was passed making Queen Victoria the longest-reigning British monarch. As if to gild her year with added lustre, the economy began to improve. International trade started to revive as the world came out of its long depression; and government expenditure showed very little increase, so that the Chancellor was able to announce an unusual surplus of nearly £8 million in his budget.

Londoners, in particular, could scarcely contain their sense of jubilation as they waited impatiently for the great day, June 22, 1897, to arrive, when premiers, potentates, and troops would come in from all corners of the globe to pay the greatest imperial tribute to a reigning monarch which had been witnessed since the days of imperial Rome. There were Victorian exhibitions at the Crystal Palace and in many other places; at the Victorian Era Show at Earl's Court, the waitresses all wore 'old English costumes'. Fashion decreed that the colour for the autumn should be purple in honour of the queen, though that royal colour was to be replaced by khaki a few years later during the Boer War. By royal command, school-children were given an extra week's holiday. Four days before the celebrations, a huge military tattoo was mounted at Windsor Castle, which the Queen watched from an upstairs window. On June 21, the Queen travelled up from Windsor to receive the homage of her ministers and of her colonial premiers at Buckingham Palace. A state banquet was held in the evening. The Queen sent a jubilee message by electric telegraph to the widespread territories of her vast empire. The jubilee celebrations and the service of thanksgiving at St Paul's Cathedral were an enormous success. The Queen rode in an open carriage through six miles of the capital's streets, lined by cheering, flag-waving crowds, followed by a colourful procession of dignitaries, troops and police from all parts of the Empire—Borneo Dyaks, Bikanir Camel Corps, Jamaica Artillery, Cypriot Zapsticks, New South Wales Lancers and many more. Punch was absolutely delighted and overcome by 'the gigantic success, for it has shown that a quarter of the world loves and appreciates a blameless Queen, and rejoices to be her subjects'.

But this imperialist fervour almost inevitably brought England into conflict with other white powers searching for new wealth in distant continents. In the following year there was great tension between England and France when Kitchener marched south from Khartoum to occupy the rest of the Sudan only to find French troops already encamped at Fashoda on the Upper Nile. After

Previous pages: Queen Victoria leaving Buckingham Palace for her Diamond Jubilee celebrations

Shortly after the Jubilee celebrations, relations between Britain and the Boers became strained again. John Bull gives the Boers a warning in plain English: 'As you *will* fight, you shall have it. *This* time it's a fight to the finish' (1899)

180

some intense diplomatic activity and hints of war, the French agreed to renounce their claim to the territory and withdrew their forces.

Disputes with the 'boring' Boers in southern Africa were of much longer standing. President Kruger of the Transvaal had been deeply suspicious of English intentions ever since the Jameson raid and had been buying large quantities of guns and other arms from Germany. Britain was aggrieved by the treatment of its own subjects working in the goldfields of the Rand, who were both heavily taxed and denied the right to vote. Despite diplomatic talks, relations between the two countries became so greatly strained that by the early months of 1899 both had started moving troops towards the border. In October the Transvaal and the Orange Free State launched an attack on the neighbouring British colonies of the Cape, Natal and Bechuanaland.

The second Boer War was another chapter in the long Victorian chronicle of military incompetence and governmental mismanagement, relieved only by some individual acts of bravery and fortitude and a final ability to muddle through. Initially, there was a strong feeling of jingoism in England and a false assumption of easy victory as there had been in the first few months of the Crimean War over half a century before. An officer addresses a young subaltern who is packing his kit before sailing for South Africa:

> *Officer:* What on earth do you want with all those polo sticks?
> *Subaltern:* Well, I thought we should get our fighting done by luncheon-time, and then we should have the afternoon to ourselves and get a game of polo!

But these hopes evaporated as quickly as dew on the sun-baked veld. Eleven years before the war broke out, Punch had been complaining that the army had only two hundred heavy guns when two thousand were needed, and that the 18,500 men and non-commissioned officers in the cavalry had to share 11,800 horses between them; but neither deficiency had been remedied before hostilities started, so that British soldiers were outgunned, and horses had to be requisitioned from transport companies and even from some county hunts. Arthur James Balfour, who held office as First Lord of the Treasury and Leader of the House of Commons under his uncle the Marquis of Salisbury, was made to confess in Punch that Kruger had taken them by surprise:

> We heard that he had got some guns,
> But only very little ones;
> We also heard of mounted forces
> *But never dreamed they rode on horses!*

The lessons of the first Boer War of 1881 had still not been learnt and the army, which was usually adequate in fighting natives, was still no better equipped to deal with white sharpshooters. Volunteers rushed to join the colours, but many of them were too unhealthy and undersized for military service, as generations of poverty had ground them into genetic decline. These revelations about the condition of the submerged third in the nation shocked the conscience of the Little Englanders, led by David Lloyd George, who believed that social reform at home was more necessary than imperialist wars overseas.

Although the Boers made no deep penetrations into the British colonies, within a month they were besieging three border towns: Mafeking in Bechuanaland, Kimberley in Cape Colony, and Ladysmith in Natal. As a result of these initial setbacks, the government hastily sent out fifty thousand troops from England under the command of the sixty-year-old General Sir Redvers Buller, who had previously distinguished himself in numerous colonial campaigns. Shortly afterwards they also despatched a large consignment of armchairs for the use of officers serving in the field! Buller was less successful in fighting Boers than natives and by Christmas had suffered several heavy defeats. The government then despatched an even larger force, including contingents from Canada, Australia and New Zealand, under Lord Roberts, with Kitchener as his chief of staff. By February, 1900, the overwhelming weight of numbers had begun to reverse British fortunes. The sieges of Kimberley and Ladysmith were soon raised, and by May, Mafeking, which had been resolutely defended for seven months by Colonel R S S Baden-Powell (the founder of the Boy Scout movement), had also been relieved. The relief of Mafeking led to riotous celebrations in London, which added yet another word, mafficking, to the language.

By June it appeared that the war was practically over. The capital towns of both the Orange Free State and of the Transvaal had been taken, and Kruger had fled to seek support, unsuccessfully, from other European powers. The troops started to come home and Kitchener was left to mop up any isolated pockets of resistance; but the high command had made yet another serious

There were the same inappropriate supplies of clothing in the Boer War as there had been in the Crimean War. The original caption read: 'Fat, Sir! Law bless ye, no, Sir! It's Christmas presents from 'ome, Sir. Cardigan jackets, flannin' hunder-wear, hall-wool socks, an' cellerar. Got 'em hall on. Bullet-proof to-day, Sir!' (1900)

A LESSON FROM THE FRONT

When a commander asks for a truce, apparently for no particular reason, consent at once and give him his own time.

While the truce continues, have the delicacy not to inquire into the movement of your opponents.

Remember that firing on ambulances and quarters reserved for women and children may have been the outcome of a mistake.

Force upon the opposing general plenty of leisure for removing all his forces, including his heavy guns.

And then, when you find your bird flown, men, horses and artillery disappeared, express intense surprise at the power of your opponent to come 'to think of such a clever thing'!

1900

Above left: 'Mafeking night, or rather 3 a.m. the following morning' (1900)

Above right: The division between social classes was strikingly revealed in this cartoon. The lady asks the street urchin if he could eat one of the cakes in the window. He replies 'Why, I'd heat six on 'em' (1900)

error of judgment, for this operation took much longer than had been anticipated. Under determined and skilful leaders, such as de Wet, Botha and Smuts, the Boers conducted a long guerilla campaign against the British forces and did not finally surrender until May 31, 1902.

Victoria, who had proclaimed in the darkest days of the Boer War, 'the Queen is not interested in the possibility of defeat', did not live to see the final victory. At 6.45 pm on Tuesday, January 22, 1901, she died peacefully at Osborne after a short illness. She was eighty-one. She had reigned for sixty-three years, and had out-lived her husband, Prince Albert, by forty years, and three of her nine children. Through her own strong character and immense will-power, her dignity and her courage, she had become the apotheosis of the English people. Punch's tribute to her consisted of a series of black-bordered cartoons, republished from earlier volumes, to illustrate some of the most memorable events of her long reign, and an elegy:

O great in heart! in whom the world has known
Wisdom with woman's sweetness reconciled;
Who held her kingdom's honour, as her own,
Still fair and undefiled!

Best shall they keep that shameless memory
Who count their heritage a holy debt, bright
Who walk with fearless soul the way of light
In which her feet were set.

'The Roll of Great Monarchs.
History adds another name' (1901)

10 EPILOGUE

With its thirty-thousand, double-column, closely-printed pages—an inimitable record of the reign—Punch became just as an essential part of the Victorian age as carriages and coaches, white-aproned servants, and the Albert Memorial. It had its detractors, and its imitators, like *Judy* and *Fun*, which introduced itself in 1861 with almost the same message as Punch had used twenty years before: 'Now to make the first joke, the pioneering pun, the crashing conundrum.' Both of these rival magazines lasted for forty years, but Punch went on for ever.

Punch survived because it moved with the times, and helped, in part, to create them. In our nostalgic envy, we may imagine that Queen Victoria's long reign was settled and secure, but Punch soon disabuses us of that belief; indeed, it was only royal longevity which deceptively gave those years the apparent unity of an age. Year after year, decade after decade, generation after generation, Punch expressed the changing views and moods of its readers more trenchantly, more outspokenly, more funnily than they could ever have done themselves.

Punch drew its strength from daily life. The cartoons by such great artists as John Leech, Sir John Tenniel, Charles Keene, George du Maurier, Phil May, to mention only a few of the more prominent, did not make their point by American exaggeration of outline but by reproducing, often in the minutest detail, verisimilitude. We can still sense that many of the recorded incidents could have occurred in real life or actually did; indeed, we are sometimes assured of that latter truth in the caption. At its best, the humour is universal and enduring. The foxed and yellowed pages can still lighten today's lips with a smile and raise many a laugh, though guffaws may be heard less frequently now than they doubtless were in those long, black and boring nights when paterfamilias pondered over each page for hours by oil or gas light.

Punch also survived because it was so very English. There is nothing which is so redolent of the English character with all its virtues, vices and inconsistencies. Punch was just and honest within its intellectual limitations; chauvinistic in the face of foreigners, but inclined to be either too smug or too despondent at home; kind, and even compassionate, where its own dogmatic prejudices were not involved. It was irreverent, independent, incorruptible, and no respecter of persons, pretensions or place-seekers wherever they were to be found. For countless years it waged campaigns against self-seeking MPs, the officer caste, post-office inefficiency, speculation, bumbledom, vested interests and social pretensions, yet, in the end, to little real effect. How many of its lost causes still haunt us to this day like Victorian ghosts!

If England lost its way, it did so in Victorian times. As the greatest historian of that age, G M Young, wrote in his classic *Victorian England, Portrait of an Age*:

> But, fundamentally, what failed in the late Victorian age, and its flash Edwardian epilogue, was the Victorian public, once so alert, so masculine, and so responsible. Compared with their fathers, the men of that time were ceasing to be a ruling or a reasoning stock; the English mind sank towards that easily excited, easily satisfied state of barbarism and childhood which press and politics for their own ends fostered.

The crisis of confidence, the lack of nerve and of will, is made manifest in the pages of Punch. Like many other Victorians, Punch was never able to turn away wrath into the more productive channels of a modern philosophy. Instead, it retreated into a somewhat nihilistic sense of disillusion with technological civilization, which had been apparent in Punch from the very start. In the end it preferred laughter to effort or philosophy. That laughter still echoes over the intervening century to mock our endeavours of the present day.

Previous page: Edward VII on horseback follows the gun carriage during Queen Victoria's funeral procession

ACKNOWLEDGEMENTS

The author and publishers would like to thank Punch for supplying all the cartoons used in this book, and the following agencies for supplying the illustration used on the pages listed:

Mansell: 6, 36, 60, 106, 132, 178, 186
Radio Times Hulton Picture Library: 82, 146, 162

INDEX